RELOADING TOOLS, SIGHTS, AND TELESCOPES FOR SINGLE SHOT RIFLES

By
Gerald O. Kelver

Books on Single Shot Rifles by the same author:

Major Ned H. Roberts and The Schuetzen Rifle – 1951

Schuetzen Rifles – History and Loadings – 1972

*100 Years of Shooters and Gunmakers of
Single Shot Rifles* – 1975

Respectfully Yours – H. M. Pope – 1976

3rd Edition © 1998
Pioneer Press,
Union City, TN

ACKNOWLEDGEMENTS

All photographs which appear in this book, except as noted, were photographed by the author.

Except as noted, all the photographic record was made from items in the author's possession at the time the photographs were made.

To all those who permitted me to photograph materials from their collections I wish to again extend my thanks for their help.

My appreciation also to the typist, Christina Brogan, Evergreen, Colorado, who so ably put this material into presentable form.

Appreciation is expressed for the help of the Arapahoe Regional Library, Littleton, Colorado and the Clinton-Essex-Franklin Library of Plattsburg, N.Y., as well as the *American Rifleman*, National Rifle Association, Washington, D.C.

To others who helped along the way you have not been forgotten because compiling information for such a manuscript as this must come from many bits and pieces.

Finally my thanks to Charles R. Suydam, Azusa, California, for his suggestions and review of the material.

Gerald O. Kelver
Brighton, Colorado

CONTENTS

FOREWORD

It was somewhat of a surprise to me to realize that the John Unertl Company of Pittsburgh, Pennsylvania is one of the last optical companies in the United States still producing externally adjustable precision target telescopes. The United States at one time was known for its precision target telescopes, but now those telescopes have been replaced by the internal adjustable rifle scope.

The old hand reloading tools used during the last 100 years are now no longer tools, but collectors' items. Because of the disuse, many shooters today do not know what the tools were used for. Iron precision tang sights and target telescopes are curiosities.

Since I am of an era when these things were used, my knowledge, coupled with research, has resulted in this book. I have not included all the makers who might have produced some type of reloading tool, or telescope, for individual research will turn up many more than those I have listed. I believe, however, that the information I have presented will at least provide a basic understanding of these accessories.

My wife and I used to shoot in the muzzleloading matches at Friendship, Indiana, when the founders of the National Muzzle Loading Rifle Association were still organizing and operating the matches. I have counted as my friends many of the people who were leaders in the target shooter's world, men who were writers and gunsmiths and barrel makers.

Perhaps in some small way I can contribute to the knowledge of the past through this book.

Gerald O. Kelver

CHAPTER 1

RELOADING TOOLS

Although reloading tools have been generally treated as of secondary importance to the rifles of yesterday, this was not the actual case. Fired ammunition required that the cases be reloaded. The need remained for reloading the empty cartridge case into a usable, fully loaded cartridge. This need could only be met by manufacturing low cost hand-held tools to supply the requirements of that particular time and place, and so the reloading tools were as important as the gun itself. Schuetzen rifle tools were especially made for specialized use in reloading directly at the shooting bench.

Today, shooters consider reloading cartridge cases as having a recreational value. In the period from 1870 to 1920, it was an economic need as well as a means of keeping the guns functioning when hard earned money was at a minimum.

Reloading tools were not some strange devices manufactured to delight some collector of today. Reloading tools were designed to do a simple job of reloading empty center fire cartridge cases so that one who relied upon his rifle or revolver could use the gun in "tomorrow's" work.

The most popular reloading tool from 1884 to 1940 was the tong tool developed and patented by J. H. Barlow. The Ideal Manufacturing Company of New Haven, Connecticut was formed to manufacture these tools.

J. H. Barlow was born in England in 1846 and came to the United States when a child. He grew to adulthood and during the Civil War he became Sergeant of Company D, 14th United States Infantry of the Army of the United States. Barlow was much interested in encouraging individual marksmanship. He felt that shooting not only provided a real interest for the individual, but it also encouraged preparedness in the event of national need. For thirteen or fourteen years after the war he worked for the Winchester Repeating Arms Company as a practical mechanic. During the time he spent at Winchester, he made small tools, dies, punches, model bullets, and anything required in the manufacture of cartridges. Finally he decided to go into the production of reloading tools on his own, and the Ideal Manufacturing Company was formed.

At the same time, the J. M. Marlin Firearms Company manufactured reloading tools for their rifles as did the Winchester Repeating Arms Company, the Bullard Repeating Arms Company, the Remington Arms Company, and individual gunsmiths.

The tong type hand tools were simple to operate and low in price, so they became the standard in reloading tools from 1874 to the 1930's. After World War 1 bench model reloading tools were developed for home loading use.

The Pacific Gun Sight Company was one of the first companies to manufacture and offer for sale the "C" shaped lever tool mounted on a bench and making use of individual and replaceable die sets.

Belding and Mull, Incorporated of Phillipsburg, Pennsylvania, marketed a bench mounted straight line lever action reloading tool.

Modern Bond Corporation also made reloading tools, but they were best known for their bullet molds. The Modern Bond bullet molds had mold blocks which detached from the handles for interchangeability. This feature became standard for the Ideal Manufacturing Company molds at a much later date. Molds today are manufactured with handles that feature interchangeable mold blocks.

There were many others who, during the 1930's and 1940's, developed and sold reloading tools. For the ordinary shooter it was still the old Ideal tong tools that were used.

After World War II, interest in reloading increased tremendously, and unprecedented demands were made for reloading tools. The Ideal tool orders at the Lyman Gun Sight Company offices increased at such a rate in the period immediately following the war that they were shipping more in one day than they had in months before the war. Within a short time, the forces of economy and industrial expediency forced the abandonment of the old Ideal malleable iron tool with its nickeled finish.

Today's Ideal tong tool, while performing all the reloading operations as in the past, is certainly no beauty and just doesn't have the feeling of the old time tools. Perhaps this is simply nostalgia on my part. On the other hand, there was nothing worse than trying to cast bullets from a mold attached to the nickeled cast iron handles of a tong tool. The only way that I have found to make the attached mold usable is to friction tape several layers on the handles and then cover it with adhesive tape. Even then I wear a lined leather glove on the left hand to make the heat bearable. These molds and tools must be hot before you can cast good bullets, and the heat must be maintained.

The hand held reloading tool competiton was over by 1900, and within a short time the field was left entirely to the Ideal Manufacturing Company.

The Winchester Repeating Arms Company reloading tools were tong tool adaptations. Only a limited number of certain tools of the Winchester reloading tool line proved popular.

Ballard-Marlin tools were not extensively used although they were well made. The original hand reloader made by Marlin was based on a patent of John Browning of Utah. Later when the Marlin Firearms Company took over the Ideal Manufacturing Corporation, the Marlin tools as distinctive items were dropped, and the Marlin name became a part of the Ideal trademark.

Many individual gunsmiths across the United States made reloading tools of various types to serve their customers. None of these became popular items beyond their own areas; however, they do provide an interest to today's collectors. Some of the devices are very ingenious and others but crude attempts to make something that would work.

Some molds are found with numbers and unusual markings on them. These variations may have been put on the tools by the maker, or in the intervening years they may have been put on by some owner. Who knows? The variation always lends spice to the chase, for one can never say that these are the facts because there's always the variant to be dealt with.

CHAPTER 2

IDEAL RELOADING TOOLS

The first patent J. H. Barlow received was for a *Cartridge Implement*, December 23, 1884. This patent was for the basic tong tool with an adjustable chamber, a case resizer, and re-primer. On June 11, 1889, a patent was issued to Francis J. Rabbeth, a well known shooter of the time, for a measuring powder flask. This device was cylindrical in shape and contained some unusual inside mechanism. The patent was made available to J. H. Barlow, and the powder flask was manufactured as one of the Ideal tool accessories. This was the first commercially produced powder measure.

Later patents were issued to Barlow for tools in common use during the Schuetzen shooting days. On February 10, 1891, he received a patent for an adjustable bullet mold. This mold was devised to make a mold available to the shooter which would cast different weight bullets of the same caliber without the expense of different size molds. This mold was manufactured by the Ideal Company as the *Perfection Mold.*

On December 1, 1891, Barlow received a patent for a tong type hand held bullet sizer. This device, which operated on the principle of the pliers of today, had a removable die in the handle grip part which could be removed and another size substituted.

On November 22, 1892 he received a patent for a pocket pliers de-capping tool with a projecting, removable de-capping pin. This simple tool could be used very handily at the shooting bench for the removal of the fired primer and the reinstallation of a new primer. This made the Schuetzen style of shooting practical and the reuse of one cartridge case which was fire formed to the chamber of that particular rifle possible.

There were other patents, but these are several of the patents most noteworthy to the single shot rifle shooter. John H. Barlow readily accepted ideas to improve his product, and he was always ready to accept suggestions from the shooters. When new bullet forms were suggested, he made cherries and cut new molds.

Homer Kephart suggested bullet forms for the .25 and .30 calibers. Harry M. Pope and Dr. W. G. Hudson suggested bullet forms for the .25 and .32 calibers. C. H. Herrick designed .22, .25, and .28 caliber bullet forms. Mr. Beardsley of the Bridgeport Gun Implement Company suggested .30 caliber bullets. The U.S. Marine corps used Ideal molds which they designed for .30/40 match shooting. This list is not complete, but does give one an idea of the suggestions which Mr. Barlow received and used.

Ed P. Bernard of Yokohama, Japan, designed the spire case bullets used in the .25 caliber as well as the 7mm Mausers. C. C. Crossman of the St. Louis, Misouri, Revolver Club designed revolver bullets, and W. H. French, the noted Schuetzen sharpshooter, designed a bullet with bands of different diameters and having a spire point for the .32/40.

The Hudson, French, and Pope-Stevens bullets all require special throating in the barrel so that they will seat properly. Each of these bullets has the bands cast in different diameters so that the bullet may be called "tapering". This taper insures the bullet seating concentric to the bore. If the throating of the barrel is not done, these bullets will seat so hard that the bullet will be deformed and lose the built-in accuracy.

C. W. Rowland, the famous rifle shot of Boulder, Colorado, demonstrated what could be done with these bullets in an article published February 22, 1906, in *Shooting and Fishing* published by the National Rifle Association.

In *Ideal Handbook No. 23* published in 1910, Dr. Walter G. Hudson of New York City contributed five pages of information as a result of his experiences. The article refers in detail to making the .32-40 and the .38-55 calibers shoot at their very finest. One surprising point that Dr. Hudson made was that smokeless powder loads gave him average daily scores that were consistently better than his muzzle loaded black powder scores. He notes that he keeps his muzzle loading rifles "for the sake of the pleasant memories associated with them". (Remember, this was in 1910).

Mr. Barlow, who had formed the Ideal Manufacturing Company based on his 1884 patent, announced his retirment and sale of the company to the Marlin Firearms Company on May 16, 1910. The Marlin Firearms Company continued the manufacture of the Ideal tools under their name until 1915 when the company was taken over by the Marlin-Rockwell Corporation. At this point in time things get a little hazy. Although there are no official records, some writers insist that the Winchester Repeating Arms Company bought the Ideal Manufacturing part of the Marlin Firearms Corporation. Winchester had already taken a positive stand against cartridge reloading and had stopped the sales of their own reloading tools, so it hardly seems reasonable that they would have bought the Ideal Manufacturing Company.

In my research of Harry M. Pope's own files, I found substantiated evidence that the Ideal Manufacturing Company was purchased and operated by a friend of Mr. Pope, a Phineas M. Talcott. The purchase occurred around 1916. In December, 1925, Mr. Pope wrote a letter which indicates the sale of the Ideal Manufacturing Company to the Lyman Gun Sight Company as of October, 1925. The full report of this transaction appears in my book *Respectfully Yours, H. M. Pope*.

The Lyman Gun Sight Company continued the manufacture and sale of the Ideal reloading tools in the tradition established by J. H. Barlow. The days of the hand held tong tool are numbered by simple economics if nothing else, for as the increased cost of manufacturing is passed on to the consumer, the price differential between the hand held tool and the more sophisticated bench tool becomes less. As demand lessens, manufacturing costs increase. The result is that an uneconomical product is dropped.

The Ideal reloading tong tools were issued and identified by numbers. The series ran from No. 1 through No. 10. I also have a .25-35 transition tool which is the tong tool with detachable mold, the same as used on the later wooden detachable handles made for the interchangeable mold blocks.

Ideal #1 tool was nickel plated and had two blocklike projections which extended beyond the tool. These blocks were drilled to hold the case and were used as the re-capper in the early models. There was no bullet sizer on this model since it was made for "heel bullets" which could not be crimped. Made for revolver cartridges in .22 C.F., .32, .38, and .41, the re-capper was on the handle in later manufactured tools.

Ideal #2 - single adjustable chamber for adjusting to bullet seating depth. Mold attached to handles. Re-capper extended beyond mold. Bullet sizing hole in handle. Made for target pistol reloading in Smith and Wesson calibers .32-44 and .38-44.

Ideal #3 - had no mold but did have a die set to be used with the handles which consisted of a muzzle resizer (now known as a "neck resizer") and a single adjustable chamber. This was made for all straight taper rimmed rifle cartridges from .22-20 Hornet to .45-90 W.C.F. including Stevens, Colt, Marlin, Sharps, Remington, Ballard, Bullard, U.S. Government, Maynard, and Winchester cartridges. This tool could also be furnished to seat paper patched bullets.

Ideal #4 - mold attached; made for a .22-20 Hornet, .32 Ideal, .25-20 repeater and single shot, and for pistol cartridges. The loading chamber was a fixed part of the handle. The re-capper was in the handle part as was the bullet sizing hole with plunger.

Ideal #5 - made only for the .45 U.S. Government. Blocks extended beyond the handles and were machined for a re-capper and case re-sizer. The handle part had a non-adjustable chamber and a bullet sizing hole and plunger. A double adjustable chamber for the 500 grain bullet could be screwed into the block where the re-sizing die was located.

Ideal #6 - mold blocks were attached to the handles. There was a non-adjustable chamber. The re-capper and bullet sizing hole with plunger were on the handles. The tool was made for grooved bullets. Made for rimmed black powder cartridges from .25-35 to .50-100-450. One cartridge was the .42-77-370 Berdan Russian. Cartridges over 2½ inches in length had adjustable chambers, since this was the limit on the length of the fixed chamber.

Ideal #7 - no mold attached, fixed loading chamber, re-capper on handle. Made only for the reloading of .44 X.L. shot cartridges used in Colt Lightning rifles and Marlin .44 Caliber 1889.

Ideal #8 - special mold blocks attached to the handles. Had a base cavity former attached to inside of mold. Fixed chamber in handle as well as re-capper. The bullet sizing plunger is not rounded, but is formed to fit the base of the bullet. Made for .32, .41, .450, and .455 British revolver cartridges.

Ideal #9 - at present no information is available regarding this tool.

Ideal #10 - made for grooved rimless cartridges. No mold.

Uses a set of dies inserted where fixed chamber was previously located on the handle. Has a pivoted priming hook which slides into groove of cartridge head to prevent rimless cartridge from movement while being primed.

After World War II, the old cast iron nickeled tools were all dropped from manufacture.

All Ideal tools have the end of the loading chamber chamfered, the idea being that this could be inserted into the case and given a twist or two to chamfer the mouth of the cartridge case so that lead cast bullets could be started into the case without shearing lead from the bullet.

Some Ideal tools were sent with a brass powder charge cup for measuring or dipping the powder load.

There are no model numbers on the Ideal tong tools - the only way to identify the model is to compare it with the above descriptions.

Today the Ideal tong tool is known as the 310 Tool and is used with an individual set of dies for each particular cartridge; full length resizing cannot be done with this tool.

In the 1880's, Francis J. Rabbeth of the Walnut Hill Rifle Club of Boston, Massachusetts, developed a cylindrical .38-55-330 grain bullet which used a paper patch and no lubrication except a lubricating wad at the base of the bullet. This development led to the issuance and sale by the Ideal Manufacturing Company of a distinctive type of mold which cast a slug for use of a paper patch. The normal factory patch used by Winchester and U.M.C. went around the bullet twice and was cut on an angle of about 25 degrees. A shooter developed a single lap patch known as the "Chase" patch with square ends which was supposed to give scores that were superior.

A series of molds in the 1880-1890's was also developed by Ideal known as the "Perfection" molds. These molds had adjustable depth rods on the mold blocks which permitted the shooter to cast bullets of a number of weights. This was done by adjusting the depth screw on the mold blocks before casting the bullets.

A. C. Gould, editor of the National Rifle Association's publication *Shooting and Fishing*, then located in New York, prevailed upon J. Barlow to make an improved .45/70 Government bullet for hunting, and so the .45-330 grain hollow point "Gould Express" was developed. This bullet is well adapted to a number of .45 caliber cartridges other than the .45

Government. The original .25-20-86 Single Shot was developed by the J. Stevens Arms and Tool Company. The .25-20-86 Repeater was developed by th Ideal Manufacturing Company for the Marlin Firearms Company and was later chambered by the Winchester Repeating Arms Company as the .25-20 Winchester Repeater cartridge.

The .25-20-86 Single Shot was used in a number of different single shot rifles, but was never chambered in a repeating rifle.

The .25-25-86 was developed by the Ideal Manufacturing Company at the request of Captain W. L. Carpenter of the U.S. Infantry.

The .25-21-86 was then developed from the .25-25-86.

The .32 Ideal is really a very long .32/20 case and was developed by J. Barlow of the Ideal Company. The cartridge was first made by the Union Metallic Cartridge Company. The cartridge was then chambered for a rifle by the J. Stevens Arms and Tool Company. It was also chambered in the Winchester single shot rifle. This case is simple to lathe turn, and several everlasting cases can easily be made from bar brass stock.

"Everlasting" cases are simply cases with solid head and thicker side walls than the old folded head cases.

If, in shooting, the .25/25/86 case has a neck split, do not throw it away for it can be cut off, annealed, and used in the .25/21/86. This may also account for the present scarcity of .25/25 cases, for they were commonly cut off and used in the .25/21.

Powder measures were introduced by the Ideal Manufacturing Company when Mr. Barlow first advertised the Ideal Loading Flask. This tubelike, hand held flask contained 12 ounces of black powder. The flask used a unique system of measurement within the flask. The measured powder in turn was transferred to a tube within the flask. This arrangement permitted a long powder drop into the cartridge case. The effect of this long drop was to pack the powder grains more closely in the cartridge case. This gave a more uniform charge than that permitted by the dip type charge cups used up until that time. The patent on this measure was issued to Francis J. Rabbeth on June 11, 1889, #404932.

The perfection Mold had an adjustable screw arrangement on the blocks and permitted varying the length of the grooved bullet. In the .32-40 size, this permitted making bullets from 105 grains to 210 grains.

The Perfection Mold was made for the .25-40, .25-20, .32, .32-

40 Marlin, .38, .38-55 Marlin, .40, .40 Winchester, .40 Sharps, .45-70 Standard U.S., .45 Winchester, and the .45 Sharps.

The Ideal Cylindrical Adjustable Mold was a mold made to cast bullets for paper patching. The mold had a round wood grip handle with a rod which screwed into the long cylindrical mold body. The adjusting screw permitted making the bullet to the length wanted and was also used to press out the finished cast bullet. These molds were made in .25, .32, .38, .40, and .45 calibers.

The first Ideal Universal Powder Measure with a powder reservoir and an adjustable cylindrical powder chamber operated by a handle was made under a patent of August 16, 1892. All of the tools were illustrated in the Ideal Handbook Number 7.

The No. 7 Handbook also illustrated the Ideal tong bullet sizing tool which had an interchangeable die in its handle for sizing lubricated grooved bullets. The die was mounted on a pivot and was always in alignment with the plunger which forced the bullet through the die. This tool was patented December 1, 1891, #464311.

The hand held Ideal re- and de-capper was also illustrated. The device had a changeable die in the handle which permitted using it for different cartridges. The de-capper was a removable round piece with a de-capping pin which could also be changed to fit the cartridge case. The de-capper was inserted in the cartridge case and the base was placed over a hole in the bench. Using the heel of the hand on the hinge joint, the cap was pressed out. The dies and cartridge case guide were made in all calibers from .22 to .50. This device was patented November 22, 1892, #486659.

The Ideal bullet seater was also one of the accessories advertised. This device seated the bullet into the bore of the rifle just ahead of the chamber. The seater had an adjustable plunger so that the bullet could be seated to the proper depth. The recommended setting was 1/32 of an inch ahead of the cartridge case itself.

Harry M. Pope's method of breech seating the bullet into the chamber of the rifle prior to loading the charged cartridge case in the chamber was not originated by Mr. Pope. The earliest published suggested method of breech loading the bullet first that I have found was the detailed instructions given by T. S. Van Dyke in the December 5, 1885 issue of the *American Field*.

Mr. Van Dyke wrote: "The following method I have tested most carefully and find fully equal to loading from the muzzle with a rod, giving absolute perfection.

A new, clean shell, which entirely fills the chamber is cut out behnd so as to admit a little ramrod one-half an inch or so longer than the shell. In the mouth of this shell, the ball either round or long, is patched and inserted just as it would be in the muzzle of the rifle, except that it may be pushed in flush with the edge with the thumb. This is put in the chamber, and with the little ramrod, the ball (bullet) is pushed clear of the shell into the grooves of the rifle. The empty shell is then withdrawn and one loaded with powder and wadding put in its place, and the rifle is ready. For those who load their own shells, this is the much better plan when there is no haste.

I know positively that rifles can be made to throw the best possible balls (bullets) for 100, 200, 300, and 400 yards respectively. Loaded through an empty shell as described above they have every advantage of the muzzle loader with twice the speed of loading, yet retain every advantage of the breech loader for still quicker work. Such I predict will be the rifle of the future."

The Universal Powder Measure by 1898 had become known as the Ideal #1 Measure. In 1898, the #2 had been added to the line.

The #2 was the same as the #1 with a round cylindrical powder reservoir of tin and a cylindrical adjustable crank turned measure. The #2 had a small funnel shaped powder container mounted on the leftside of the cylinder. This permitted the shooter to "Schuetzen" load, using a smokeless powder priming charge with the main charge of black powder coming from the large powder reservoir.

Ideal powder measures 3 and 4 were for loading shotgun cartridges.

On July 18, 1899, patent improvements were granted for the powder measures and the No. 1 and No. 2 measures were then identified as the Model 1899 Powder Measures. These models had an improved micrometer adjustable powder measuring chamber. Later the Number 1 and 2 Universal Powder Measures were dropped from the catalog and the #5 and #6 cast iron measures were introduced about 1904.

The #5 measure eventually became the modern #55 Ideal measure which was introduced in 1949.

The #6 measure replaced the old No. 2 measure. The #6 was a

duplex powder measure made of cast iron and having two powder chambers. On one downward stroke of the handle the priming charge was dropped into the cartridge case. On the upstroke, the main charge was measured, and on the downstroke it was dropped into the charge tube and into the case. In my opinion, regardless of the maker, the #6 Ideal powder measure was the most practical, reliable measure produced by anyone making equipment for the Schuetzen single shot rifle shooter.

Both the Number 5 and the Number 6 Ideal measures came with 2 charge drop tubes. One tube was 2 inches long and the other 7 3/4 inches long. The Number 6 powder measure was last advertised in th Number 30 Ideal Handbook of 1931.

One tool, which I have not previously mentioned, was introduced by the Ideal Manufacturing Company between 1900 and 1910. This tool was called the Ideal Shell Indentor and Fluted Cap Extracter.

The hand held plier type tool was developed to indent the cartridge case so that the bullet would rest on this indentation. The idea was to prevent irregular ignition caused by the bullet falling back onto the smokeless powder which no longer filled the case as did black powder.

Although it had limited use in single shot rifles, it was used extensively in reloading cartridges for the tubular magazine rifles such as Marlin and Winchester. The use was particularly recommended for short range practice or light charges for small game.

I have found when using this device that the indentations are blown outward by the gas formed by the powder explosion within the case, and the indentations must be reformed for the next firing. Eventually, the case ends up with four equally spaced round holes in the neck of the case.

There were two Ideal tools that were originally developed for the reloading of U.S. Government cartridges. One was the Lightning de-capper in a bench clamp hand plunger tool, and the other was a lever action straight line bench mounted tool known as the Ideal No. 2 Re- and De-Capper. This latter tool was also made for many of the single shot cartridges. The tool de-capped and re-primed the case with one stroke of the lever. The primers were fed into the machine one at a time.

I have not mentioned the No. 1 and No. 2 Ideal lubricating machine, since they are not recommended for making accurate loads for single shot rifles. The No. 1 machine was developed in 1899. The No. 2 was basically the No. 1, although more ruggedly made for Army use in reloading .30 U.S. Government cartridges.

When using a sizing machine of any kind, you subject the bullet to a shearing action that is not consistent from bullet to bullet, and fine accuracy is not possible due to the variances in the bullet.

Effective October, 1925, the Lyman Gun Sight Corporation announced that it had taken over the Ideal Manufacturing Company. At this point the two companies became one, and Lyman produced the Ideal tools from that time.

The Lyman Gun Sight Corporation no longer is owned by the Lyman family and has undergone several corporate changes since leaving the family ownership.

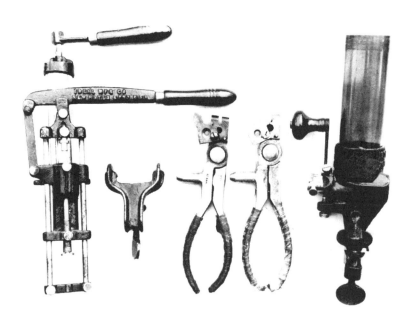

Ideal #1 Reloading Tools. Left: 1899 bullet sizer, lubricator. Middle: 1884 tong tools with molds, recapper on end of mold. Right: 1899 #1 powder measure.

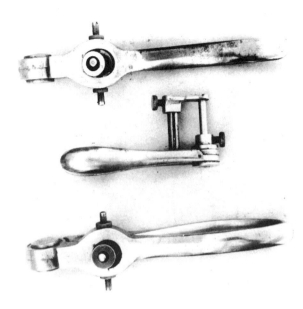

Ideal bullet sizing tools with a shell indentor in the center.

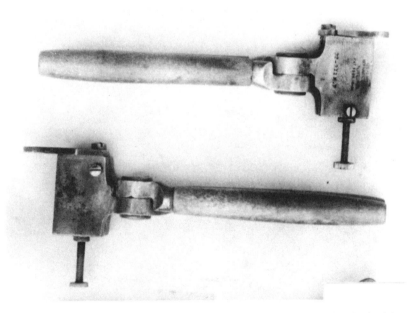

Ideal adjustable molds patented in 1891. Various bullet weights can be obtained by changing the screw adjustment.

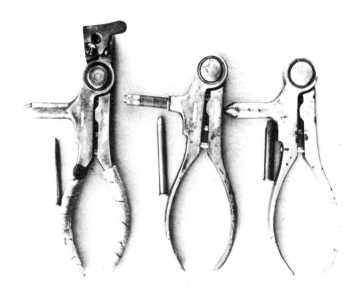

Ideal reloading tools. Left: #4 tool with attached .25-21 mold. Middle: #3 adjustable chamber tang tool for .28-30 Stevens. Right: #4 non-adjustable chamber .32 Ideal tool.

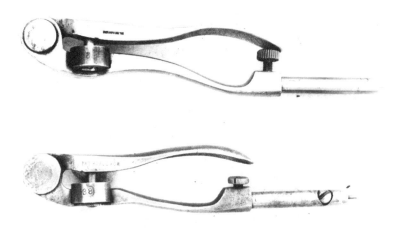

Two different types of Ideal re and de cappers.

Ideal #1 "Powder Flask" which was a successful commercially made powder measure. The original patent #404932 was issued to F. J. Rabbeth on June 11, 1889 and licensed to J. H. Barlow of the Ideal Mfg. Company.

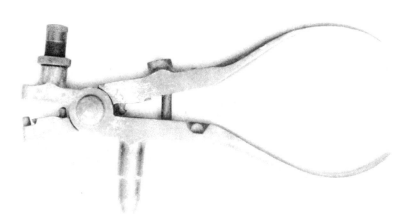

No. 1 1884 Ideal tong tool .45-60. The Berdan primer removal arm is missing. The die is for neck sizing the cartridge case. Note the position of the recapper.

Original advertisement which appeared in the Chicago Field in 1884 for the Ideal #1 reloading tool.

Old time green label Ideal box for bullet mold.

Old time Ideal green label box for Ideal #6 tool.

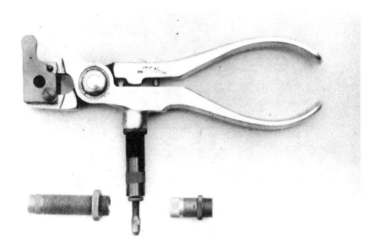

Transition Ideal .25-35 reloading tool, double adjustable chamber, neck resizer, and bullet sizing chamber. Mold blocks are removable.

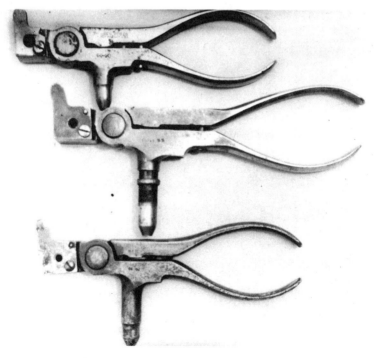

Ideal #6 reloading tools in .44-40, .40-70 Sharps straight case and .40-60. The middle tool has an adjustable chamber since the limit on fixed chambers was 2 1/2 inches.

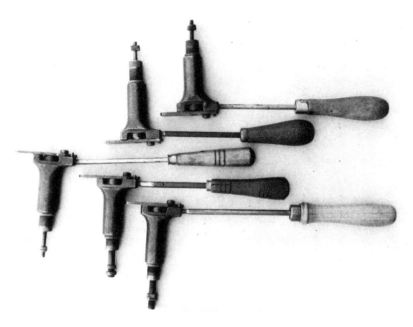

Ideal paper patch bullet molds from .25 caliber to .45. Handles are removable. Plunger depth can be regulated and also used as bullet knock out. (Patent - Jan. 10, 1893.)

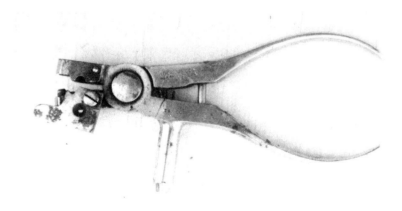

Ideal #4 reloading tool with capper on end of tool beyond the integral mold blocks. Bullet sizing die is in the handle. Chamber is fixed caliber .25-20-86 Stevens Single Shot Cartridge.

J. H. BARLOW.

CARTRIDGE IMPLEMENT.

No. 309,681.   Patented Dec. 23, 1884.

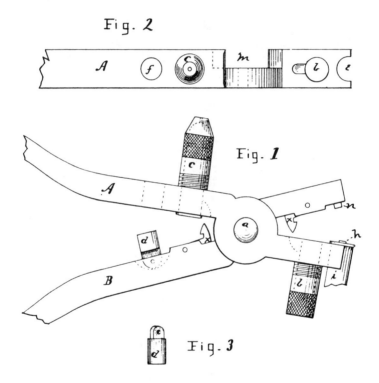

Fig. 2

Fig. 1

Fig. 3

WITNESSES:
George R. Cooley
Robert L. Hazard

INVENTOR
John H. Barlow
BY
L. S. Day
ATTORNEY

F. J. RABBETH.
POWDER FLASK.

No. 404,932.   Patented June 11, 1889.

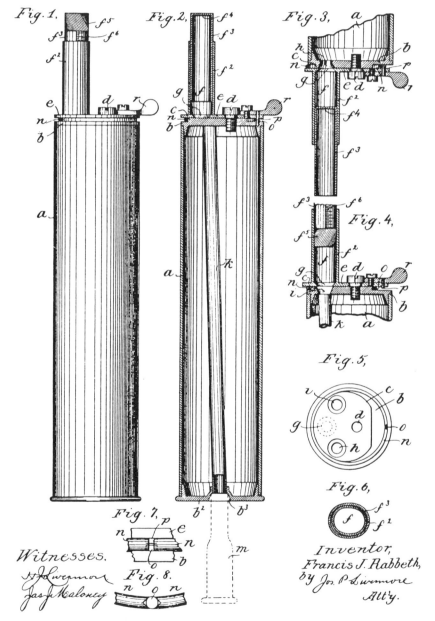

Fig. 1.

Fig. 2.

Fig. 3.

Fig. 4,

Fig. 5,

Fig. 6,

Fig. 7,

Fig. 8.

Witnesses.

Inventor,
Francis J. Rabbeth,
by Jos. P. Livermore
Att'y.

J. H. BARLOW.
BULLET MOLD.

No. 446,178.   Patented Feb. 10, 1891.

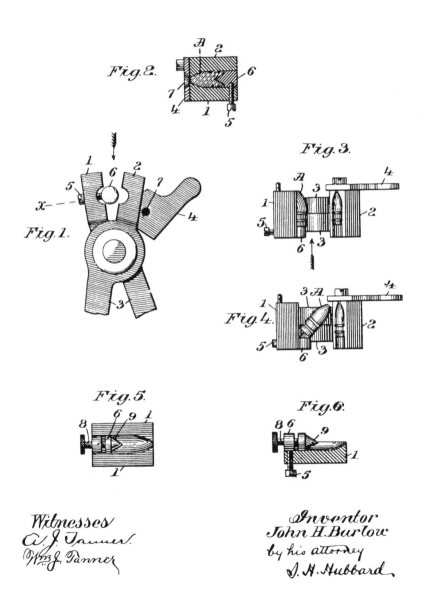

Fig.2.

Fig.1.

Fig.3.

Fig.4.

Fig.5.

Fig.6.

Witnesses
C. J. Tanner.
Wm. J. Tanner.

Inventor
John H. Barlow
by his attorney
S. H. Hubbard

J. H. BARLOW.
BULLET SIZER.

No. 464,311.   Patented Dec. 1, 1891.

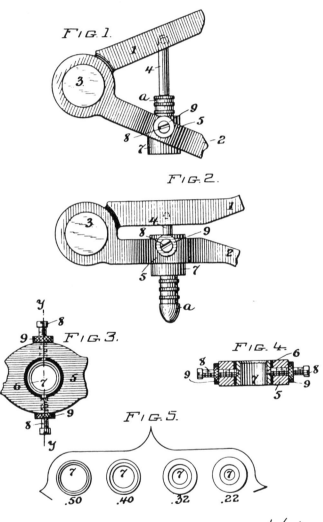

WITNESSES:
A. J. Tanner.
E. M. Newman

INVENTOR:
John H. Barlow,
by his atty.
D. H. Hubbard

J. H. BARLOW.
DECAPPING AND RECAPPING TOOL.

No. 486,659.   Patented Nov. 22, 1892.

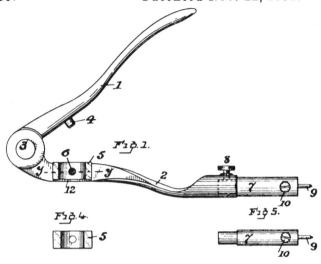

Fig. 1.

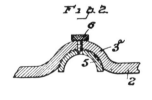

Fig. 2.

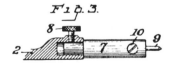

Fig. 3.

CHAPTER 3

WINCHESTER REPEATING ARMS COMPANY RELOADING TOOLS

Winchester manufactured their first tong tools under the patent date of October 20, 1874. These first tools were made to de-cap the Berdan primer first used in early American cartridge cases. Later a separate de-capping pin was provided to remove the Boxer primer which became the American standard primer. These first tools had unusual spoon shaped handles. Later a tong tool was made under a patent date of November 7, 1882. This was a well liked tool with a separate bullet mold as were all Winchester reloading tool sets.

One unusual tong tool had a double adjustable chamber with "windows" cut in the side; this was for the paper patched bullets. The marking, for example, would be 40-90 SSP which means the tool was made for the .40 caliber 90 grains of powder Sharps straight case with a paper patched bullet.

Another marking was 45 USG, meaning that the tool was made for the .45 caliber 70 grains of powder 500 grain lead bullet for the United States Government .45/70/500 cartridge.

Many of these tools are dotted with little peck like dots. These dots come from the de-capping pin which had been driven through the flash hole of the cartridge case and become hung up in the flash hole. What is more natural than just rapping the stuck pin against the tool and knocking it out of the case?

Winchester molds were made in several different patterns, but basically are the same. The main difference is in the handle or grip parts. Later molds were made with wood grips which have screws holding them on to the handles. All Winchester molds have the caliber stamped on the handle - such as 40-82. On a flat outside surface of the mold is stamped "Manufactured by Winchester Rep Arms Co. New Haven, Conn USA." The "birds head" Winchester reloading tool of February 13, 1894 is a very slow but effective tool which resizes the case as it seats the bullet. These tools had a separate de-capping pin. The chamber end of the tool has a marking such as 38-55 to denote the caliber of the tool. These tools, as are all Winchester reloading tools, are made with very fine workmanship throughout.

To use this tool, the fired cartridge case is de-primed with the separate de-capping pin (which is usually lost). Then the case is re-primed, using the lever to seat the primer. The chamber is now unscrewed. Gunpowder is measured into the cartridge case. The bullet is seated in the case with the fingers and then the whole is placed in the chamber. The chamber is screwed tight as the handle is alternately pumped until the chamber is completely screwed home. The chamber can now be unscrewed, and the full length resized formed cartridge can be removed. It is a very slow process.

The same principal was used in the long handled Winchester reloading tool of March 17, 1891. This tool is very unusual, very slow in use, and now rarely found. The handles, of which there are two, are nine inches long. One handle has the chamber screw and the other the chamber body. This tool is a full length cartridge case resizing tool. The chamber part is simply screwed together with the force necessary to reform the case. The end of the chamber has a knurled cap which can be unscrewed to open the chamber. This tool had a separate re-capping lever which is inserted in a hole in the side of the tool, and the primer is seated with a screw motion. The original re-capping lever for this tool was made with a de-capping pin in the handle end. Tools have been found with the de-capping knock out pin separate from the handle of the re-capping lever. This probably was a choice of the user, for the de-capping pin itself is easily removed from the end of the re-capping lever. The caliber of the tool is found stamped on the top flat of the screw handle.

One reloading tool which is seldom encountered is the New Model of 1888. This had a double lever arrangement and was also very slow in its use.

The Winchester reloading tools were carried in the Winchester Repeating Arms Company catalogs into the early 1900's. By catalog No. 80 of 1916, which was the 50th anniversary of the company, reloading tools were no longer advertised. In fact, Catalog No. 80 carries a warning from the company that it is impractical and dangerous to load smokeless powder, and they wished to do their "utmost to discourage this practice".

The Schoverling, Daly and Gale catalog of 1912 carried only Ideal Reloading Tools. George Tritch Hardware Company of Denver, Colorado in their 1913 catalog carried only Ideal Reloading Tools, and the Model 1894 Winchester tool with the mold sold separately and at its own price.

The Winchester catalog of 1912 cautioned shooters against reloading cartridge cases with smokeless powder, and on the last page they pictured the 1882 tong tool which they called the lever tool and stated that the 1894 tool was also available.

The calibers which they listed were from the ".22 Center Fire Single Shot" to the ".45 Sharps Patched". The calibers advertised were all straight cases or the old black powder bottle neck cases. There were no calibers listed which could be classified as modern smokeless powder types. No Winchester reloading tools were offered in subsequent catalogs and sales stopped altogether between 1912 and 1916.

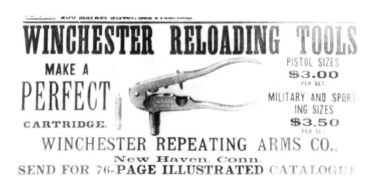

Winchester advertisement as it appeared in the May 1, 1886, issue of the American Field. Note the distinctive shape of the hinge. Model of 1880 with Berdan primer remover.

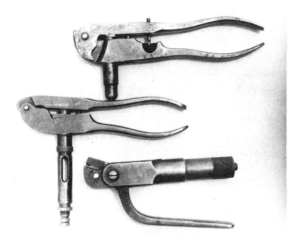

Winchester hand reloading tools. Top: .45/70/500 tong tool patent date September 14, 1880, Berdan primer remover. Middle: .40/90/330 paper patched 1882 tong tool. Tool does not crimp, made for use in single shot rifles. The adjustable chamber permits use of different bullet weights also can be used for .40/70/330. A "window" in the tool is provided so you can watch the paper patch to prevent tearing. Lower: Tool is the full length resizing reloading tool that bears the patent date of February 13, 1894. Winchester tools used a separate decapping pin which is usually lost.

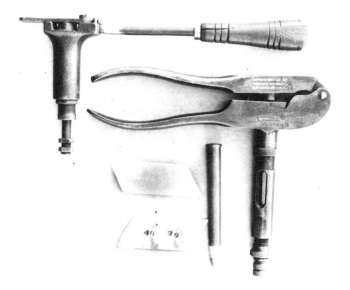

Winchester paper patch bullet reloading tool marked .40-90 SSP patented Oct. 20, 1874, Nov. 7, 1882. Ideal paper patch .40 mold patented Jan. 10, 1893. Gauge for cutting paper patch, Winchester cartridge paper patch material and .40-90 completed cartridge.

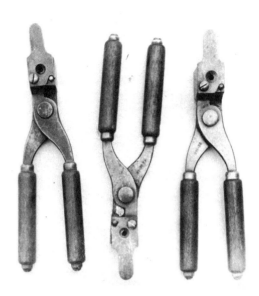

Winchester bullet molds. Plain iron handles were used until 1890. Wooden handles were used after that date. .40-82, .45-70 FP (flat point) and .32-165. Caliber is shown first, then powder charge. In the case of the .32 bullet weight is shown.

Winchester "spoon handle" reloading tools. Patented Oct. 20, 1874, Second model. .44-40 WCF and .45-70 Govt. Note the Berdan primer chisel. Tool was cast iron and gold or bronze painted.

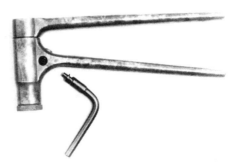

1891 Winchester full length resizer, screw handle reloading tool .32-40 with recapping rod. Patent date March 17, 1891.

Winchester blank mold for the paper patched bullet. Made for custom gunsmith who used their own bullet cherries to make a custom mold. Coll. Ed Brandhorst, Colo.

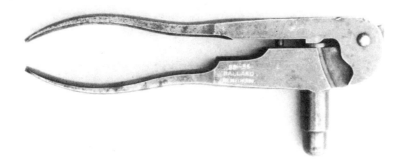

1880 Winchester tool marked .38-55 Ballard. The Marlin Ballard was the first to use the .38/55 cartridge. Coll. Richard C. Capps, Colo.

TOOLS

FOR

RELOADING CENTRAL FIRE CARTRIDGES,

MANUFACTURED BY THE

WINCHESTER REPEATING ARMS COMPANY,

NEW HAVEN, CONN., U. S. A.

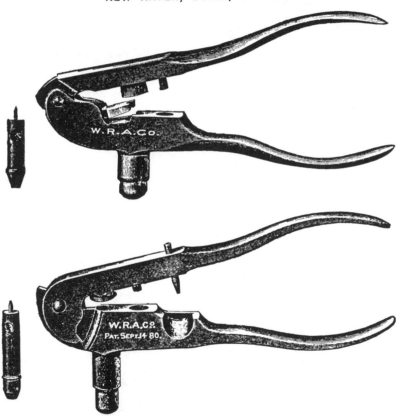

In offering these articles to the public, the manufacturers believe that they present the most complete and compact article that can be produced. The aim has been to give in one instrument all the functions possible, without complication.

As a matter of economy, many sportsmen desire to have cartridges that will reload. The shells of all our center fire rifle cartridges are made of extra thickness for this purpose. Rim fire cartridges cannot be reloaded. All shells, as soon as possible after being fired, should be cleaned and washed out carefully with strong soapsuds or soda-water, and dried thoroughly; otherwise the deposit of burnt powder left on them after firing causes them to oxidize rapidly, and they are soon destroyed. Care should be taken to set the primer well down. The pocket in the shell is always made deep enough to allow the primer to be set below the surface of the head of the shell. Premature explosions and misfires are often caused by failing to attend to this particular.

For powder to be used in rifle cartridges containing more than forty grains, we recommend the following brands and sizes of grains as giving the best results :—

American Powder Mills' "Rifle Cartridge, No. 3."
Hazard Powder Company's "Kentucky Rifle, F. G."
E. I. DuPont & Co's "DuPont Rifle, F. F. G."
Laflin & Rand Powder Co's "Orange Rifle Extra, F. F. G."

In rifle cartridges containing from twenty-five to forty grains, use one size smaller of the same brands.

In reloading the .32, .38 and .44 W. C. F. cartridges used in Winchester Model 1873 rifles, use either of the following brands and sizes ,—

American Powder Mills' "Rifle Cartridge, No. 4."
Hazard Powder Company's "Kentucky Rifle, F. F. G."
E. I. DuPont, de Nemours & Co's "DuPont Rifle, F. G."
Laflin & Rand Powder Co's "Orange Rifle Extra, F. G."

In pistol cartridges containing less than twenty-five grains two sizes smaller of the above brands will give the best results.

The American Powder Mills have just put a new brand of powder on the market, called "Rifle Cartridge Powder." This, as its name implies, is made especially for use in rifle cartridges.

Where powder is to be compressed in a shell, we earnestly recommend this brand and DuPont Rifle F. F. G. as being United States Government standard.

In such cartridges none of the high grades of powder should be used : we refer to such brands as Hazard's Electric, DuPont's Diamond Grain, etc. These powders (most excellent for use in shot-guns) owe their quick burning properties to their peculiar manufacture ; they are not hard pressed powders, and, when compressed in a cartridge shell, they cake behind the bullet more than the harder pressed brands, and give high initial pressure and very irregular shooting, without greatly increased velocity.

In casting bullets, keep the mold and lead very hot, and use the proportions of lead and tin given in the pamphlet for each bullet.

If using naked bullets, see that the grooves are filled with lubricating material ; beef tallow or Japan wax is best for this purpose. Wipe off all surplus grease before loading. When patched bullets are used, place a lubricating disc of wax with a cardboard wad both above and below it, between the ball and the powder. No wads or lubricating discs are required in reloading any of the various cartridges adapted to Winchester Rifles, or in the .45 caliber, 70 grains, Government cartridge.

Our reloading apparatus is accompanied with bullet-molds for either smooth or grooved balls, as may be ordered ; but all hand-made balls cast in this manner are comparatively imperfect, and will seldom give satisfactory results. All the bullets we use in the manufacture of cartridges are made by very heavy and perfect machinery. Balls thus made give the most accurate and satisfactory results in firing, and are constantly kept in stock.

The reloading tool, as constructed, removes the exploded primer, straightens the shell at the mouth, inserts the new primer, and fastens the ball in the shell.

A set of implements comprises the reloading tool, a bullet-mold, and charge-cup.

MODEL 1891
RELOADING TOOL.

MANUFACTURED BY THE

WINCHESTER REPEATING ARMS CO.

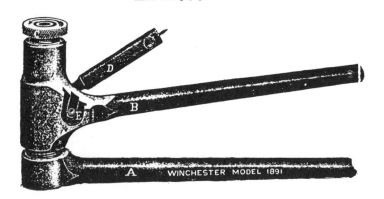

This tool extracts the spent primer, inserts the new one, reloads and resizes the cartridge. It consists of four pieces, and its use may be readily understood by examining the cut.

Part "D" (the extractor plug), is furnished with a point to knock out the primer, and serves to insert the new primer, as hereinafter described.

Part "C" is a nut with a *left-handed* screw, which is removed to place the cartridge in the die, and which is replaced to hold the same during the process of loading. It is furnished with a groove, serving to straighten the mouth of the shell.

Part "B," when turned about the die "A," by means of its handle, carries the nut "C" down upon "A," forcing the contained cartridge into the die "A."

Part "A" carries the sizing and reloading die, and is furnished with a handle as shown. This die is the vital part of the tool. The greatest care is taken to make it to the exact size and to give it a fine finish. It should be kept clean and free from rust.

This model will only be made for the following sizes of cartridges :—

32–40	45–70–405
38–55	45–70–500
38–56	45–90
40–65	50–110 Ex.
40–82	

PRICE, PER SET,   -   -   -   - $3.00.

TOOLS CAN BE FURNISHED FOR THE FOL-
LOWING SIZES OF CARTRIDGES.

22 W. C. F.	40-70 B. N. Patched.	44 Long.
32 W. C. F.	40-70 S. S. Patched.	44-77 Patched.
32 S. & W.	40-70 S. S. Grooved.	45-90 W. C. F.‡
ʾolt's.	40-70 Ballard.	45-125 Express.
ιort.	40-60 Marlin.	45-75 W. C. F.
ι ɔng.	40-60 W. C. F.	45-60 W. C. F.
32 Extra Long.	40-65 W. C. F.‡	45 Sharp's Patched.
32-40.‡	40-82 W. C. F.‡	45-70 U. S. Gov't, 405 grs.‡
38 S. & W.	40-90 B. N. Patched.	45-70 U. S. Gov't, 500 grs.‡
38 Short.	40-90 S. S. Patched.	45 Marlin.
38 Long.	40-90 Ballard.	45 S. & W.
38 W. C. F.	40-110 Express.	50 Carbine.
38-55.‡	41 Long, Colt's D. A.	50-70 U. S. Government.
38-55 W. C. F.‡	44 W. C. F.	50-95 Express.
38 Express.	44 Webley.	50-110 Express.‡
40-50 B. N. Patched.*	44 S. & W., Russian.	
40-50 S. S. Patched.†	44 S. & W., American.	

* B. N., Bottle Neck.   † S. S., Straight Shell or Sharp's Straight.
‡ The Model 1891 Reloading Tool (page 78) furnished for these Cartridges.

REDUCED PRICE LIST OF RELOADING TOOLS.

FOR RELOADING THE FOLLOWING.	RE-LOADER.	BULLET-MOLD.	CHARGE-CUP.	PER SET.
All Pistol sizes, and .32, .38, and .44 Winchester, Model 1873, . .	$1.50	$1.10	$0.10	$2.50
All Sporting and Military Cartridges,	2.00	1.10	.10	3.00
For Express Cartridges, . . .	2.00	1.70	.10	3.50

Extractor Plugs for Reloaders (any size), . . . $0.25
Swages, .38 to .44 Caliber, for smooth bullets, . . 3.00
Swages, .45 to .58 Caliber, for smooth bullets, . . 4.00
Shell-reducing dies, ... 2.00

In ordering, state what particular cartridge is to be reloaded, as only one size can be reloaded with a single set.

The majority of cartridges require no wads in reloading. For such cartridges as require wads, a wad-cutter will be added to the set at an addition of 50 cents to above prices.

Winchester Model 1894 Reloading Tool.

The Winchester Model 1894 Reloading Tool was devised to make the reloading and resizing of large sporting ammunition more easy.

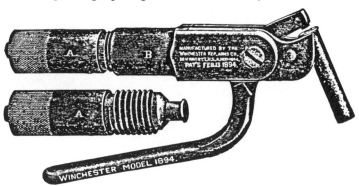

By a strong lever, a small motion (not more than .03 of an inch) is imparted to the slide. The cartridge is contained in the die A, as shown in the cut. The die screws into the frame. The shell, with its charge and bullet, is put together by hand and put into the die A. The die is screwed into the frame as far as it will go readily. A motion of the lever toward the die will force the cartridge into the die through a short distance. The backward motion of the lever releases the pressure on the cartridge, and the die can then be screwed up through a part of one turn. The repeated motion of the lever, and the continued screwing up of the die, bring the cartridge its full length into the die, insert the bullet to the right distance, crimp the cartridge around the bullet, and reduce the shell to its original size, so that it will go freely into the gun.

With this tool it will be found possible to easily reload the largest cartridges, compressing the powder, putting the bullet to place, and reducing the shell on the outside to its original form. By the reverse motion, that is, by lifting the handle of the lever away from the die, the slide is lifted, and the cartridge, by means of the extractor, is drawn a slight distance out of the die. When the handle is returned to the die, the latter can be unscrewed a corresponding distance. Another motion of the lever draws the cartridge still further out of the die, and with a few motions it becomes so loosened in the die that the latter may be easily unscrewed. As soon as the cartridge is loosened in the die, the extractor loses its grip, and the die and cartridge are taken from the frame together. This tool, new in principle, permits, with the use of little force, the most exact reloading, including the resizing of the shell.

This model will be furnished for reloading the following cartridges:—

.25-35 Winchester.	.38-72 Winchester.	.45-70 Model 1886.
.30 Winchester.	.40-60 Winchester.	.45-70-330 Model 1886.
.30 Win. Short Range.	.40-60 Marlin.	.45-70-350 Model 1886.
.32 Winchester Special.	.40-65 Winchester.	.45-70-405 U. S. Govt.
.303 Savage.	.40-70 Winchester.	.45-70-500 U. S. Govt.
.30 Army.	.40-72 Winchester.	.45-70 Marlin.
.30 Army Short Range.	.40-82 Winchester.	.45-125 Express.
.32-40.	.42 Berdan.	.50 Carbine.
.32-40 Short Range.	.43 Spanish.	.50-70 Musket.
.38-55.	.44-77 Patched.	.50-95 Express.
.38-55 Short Range.	.45-60 Winchester.	.50-100-450 Winchester.
.38-56 Winchester.	.45-75 Winchester.	.50-110 Express.
.38-70 Winchester.	.45-90 Winchester.	

Winchester Repeating Arms Co., New Haven, Conn. 1909 catalog.

CHAPTER 4

RIFLE SIGHTS

The sighting equipment on rifles evolved from a simple pin type front sight, a U notched rear, and finally to the finely graduated adjusted micrometer sight and the micrometer adjusted target telescope.

In the flintlock and percussion days the standard sighting equipment was a silver blade front sight and a V notch rear sight. In the 1850's, when the Swiss and German immigrants started shooting the offhand Schuetzen style rifles, rear sights moved back to the tang of the rifle.

Along with the development and patents of various rifle actions came a whole series of patents for sighting equipment. Because of the need, the excellence of design, and good workmanship, certain individuals became known for the sights they made.

Wm. Lyman of Middlefield, Connecticut and George and Frank Freund of Denver, Colorado and Cheyenne, Wyoming Territory were especially active in the period dating from the 1870's. After the Freund Brothers broke up their partnership in Cheyenne, Frank Freund continued to manufacture and sell sights from his new address of 912 Bergen Avenue, Greenville, New Jersey. George Freund continued making sights at his shop in Durango, Colorado.

Deane W. King of Denver, Colorado and later San Francisco, California had sights and powder measures made and sold under his name and patent rights. Still later the King rifle sights were, made by Marble Arms and Manufacturing Company of Gladstone, Michigan which incorporated some of the designs into their own line of metallic sights. King had John Redfield of

Denver make up many of his sights, and Redfield also manufactured sights under his own name and as The Western Gun Sight Company.

Later, when telescopic equipment became available, companies like Wm. Malcolm, Bausch & Lomb Optical Company of Rochester, New York; J. W. Fecker, Pittsburgh, Pennsylvania; T. M. Sidle, Philadelphia, Pennsylvania; Stevens Arms Company, Chicopee Falls, Massachusetts; Winchester Repeating Arms Company, New Haven, Connecticut; R. Noske, San Carlos, California; became known for their products along with many others whose names have not been mentioned.

During the long range and Schuetzen rifle matches the companies in the forefront who produced well made iron sights were the Remington Arms Company of Ilion, New York; the Winchester Repeating Arms Company of New Haven, Connecticut; the J. Stevens Arms Company of Chicopee Falls, Massachusetts; and the Wm. Lyman Company of Middlefield, Connecticut.

The Winchester Repeating Arms Company made sights for other arms companies to their specifications as well as for arms of their own manufacture. Remington Arms Company sights were known for their ruggedness, dependability, and reliability. The Winchester sights were finely made, accurate and reliable. Lyman sights, while made under the control of the Lyman family, have always been made with a high quality of workmanship, and the same could be said of the King, Freund, and Stevens sights.

Certainly there has been a variety of sighting equipment available to the shooter over the years. This variety has steadily led to improvement of target results as well as improved reliability in the game field.

One fallacy, however, which persists today among the general public is that a telescope will improve the accuracy of a firearm. This statement is false! A rifle telescope will enable a person to see better, but the accuracy of a firearm is built into the gun itself and no appendage added or subtracted to a firearm can change that!

This also brings up another point; many collectors of single shot rifles will not buy or will discount a rifle that has had holes drilled and tapped for telescopic target mounts! The reasoning for this is an utter mystery to me, for telescopes are a part of the sighting equipment of the rifle! Either the rifle had to have screws to hold the telescope mounts to the rifle or else they had to be put into grooves cut into the barrels as was the case with a Pope, Schoyen, Stevens, Peterson, Malcolm and the Mann-Niedner Mount.

Whether you are a bench rest shooter of today or a confirmed Schuetzen shooter, you can only hit what you can see. While this same adage applies to open or peep sights, the refinement of what you see depends upon its resolution, and that can only be provided with a sight that enables the shooter to see precisely the object he is shooting at.

Collectors are always seeking perfection in their firearms choices, not for the gun itself, but in answer to a need in their own motivation. Rifles in a perfect state of preservation are not the rifles that made the records on the rifle ranges. It was only the well used and adapted rifle that made the excellent scores which the real shooter demanded. The proof of the rifle was in the shooting, not its unmarred beauty.

In regard to sights, it might be well to mention that Morocco leather cased sights sets which are so avidly sought after by today's collectors were not furnished by only one company, such as Winchester, but were made a part of the accessory items by all companies which made long range rifles. The cases which contained the sights were made by several New York firms who also made cases for tintype photographs, etc. The inside compartments which were usually covered with a red, blue or purple velvet cloth covering were made of either gutta-percha or papier-mache. These compartments were made to hold the windgauge front sight with its inserts as well as the vernier stems of the mid-range or long-range sight. Some cases contained just the front sight and the one vernier rear sight. The sights were made by the companies making the rifles. The cases were contracted for. The name of the rifle company was stamped on the outside.

Cased target sights are known for all the standard firearms manufacturing companies as well as the lesser known companies including a few individual makers.

Almost all gunmakers at some time or another experimented with making a sight that incorporated some individual idea. Unless the sight was reproduced in some numbers it is and will remain an individual curiosity. This also applies to telescopes for they were made by individual gun makers such as A. O. Niedner, Axel W. Peterson, Arthur Hubalek and others. These telescopes, few in number, again are an expression of the individual effort.

The first successful commercially produced adjustable tang windguage sight was the Lyman No. 15 sight patented August 23, 1887.

The sight was adjustable both for windage and elevation and had a micrometer adjusting scale with one quarter minute clicks.

The sighting peep was within an eye cup or disc which was threaded and removable.

This sight could not be folded down on the tang and did not become popular.

The No. 15 sight was discontinued by the Lyman Gun Sight Company in 1906.

CHAPTER 5

TELESCOPES USED ON SINGLE SHOT RIFLES

BUCKEYE TELESCOPE
In 1886, R. C. Rice of Warren, Ohio, offered to make target and hunting rifle telescopes to order.

The number of the telescopes made is unknown. I personally have never seen one of the scopes or the mounts. The markings are unknown.

RURAL MANUFACTURING CO. RIFLE TELESCOPES
The Rural Manufacturing Co. of 44 North Fourth St.,Philadelphia, Pennsylvania, advertised and made full length rifle telescopes.

The company was continuing the optical business of Milton P. Pierce who manufactured rifle telescopes for Union sharpshooters during the American Civil War.

The tubes of the rifle telescopes were made from seamless cast steel tubes. The lens system was fixed adjustment and universal focus with rugged double screw lens mountings to permit use of the telescope with heavy charges.

The front mount was a solid ring attachment, and the rear was a screw elevation adjustment mounted on the tang of the rifle.

These telescopes were used on muzzle loading guns and Sharps 1874 models.

They are not often seen on breech loading target rifles.

THE DUPLEX TELESCOPE SIGHT
LAWSON C. CUMMINS, MONTPELIER, VERMONT

This telescope had an achromatic optical system mounted in a steel tube. The tube was ¾" and was made in tube lengths from 15 inches to 32 inches long.

The elevation and windguage movement was inside the tube and had two knurled thumb screws on the side of the tube for adjustment. The mounts were dovetailed into the barrel and were rigid.

Some of the telescopes were made with just elevation adjustment, for the windgauge adjustment was extra.

This telescope was also made in a ½" tube for pistols and light rifles.

The telescope was offered for sale in the late 1800's and early 1900's.

LYMAN GUNSIGHT CORPORATION

The Lyman Company purchased the tools and rights to manufacture the Winchester Repeating Arms Company A5 rifle telescope and mount in 1928.

The company' also bought the Stevens Arms Company telescope business in 1929. When the 1978 Centennial rifle telescope was issued with the Lyman-Ruger Centennial Rifle, the optics were from the original Stevens stock materials purchased in 1929.

The Winchester A5 became the Lyman 5A, and the Stevens telescope became the Lyman 438 Field Rifle Telescope. Lyman rifle telescopes were first advertised in 1929.

The optics used in the Lyman rifle telescopes were furnished by the Bausch and Lomb Company until 1945. The supplier later became the Plummer Precision Optics Company.

The 5A was made in 5 power, and the 438 Field telescope was made in 3 power. A 22 Junior Field scope was made in 2½ power. The target spot telescopes developed by Lyman were improved versions of the standard Lyman 5A telescope. These telescopes came to dominate the range rifles for they were excellent telescopes.

All the target rifle telescopes made by the old Lyman Company had external micrometer adjustments and utilized the dovetail bases for mounting on the rifle except for the 22 Junior Field scope which used a special mount.

The Lyman 22 Junior Field Scope in a straight ¾″ tube in 2½X magnification used Bausch and Lomb lenses. The telescope was introduced in 1935 and was discontinued in 1936.

In 1936 the ¾″ straight tube 4X Lyman 422 Expert Scope was introduced. This telescope used click target type mounts and was suitable for rifles up to the .22 Hornet. Many of these scopes were used on single shot rifles using moderate loads. The scope was discontinued when the company converted to government work at the beginning of World War II.

For accurate shooting, the centers of the telescope bases should be 7.2 inches apart. A lesser or greater distance between the two base centers will not permit exactly 1 degree of angle adjustment on the telescope itself.

The 5A Winchester mounts were machined of steel, and the machined mounts were continued as a part of the Lyman production as well.

LYMAN TELESCOPIC SIGHTS

Model No.	Years of Mfg.	Power	Tube	Tube Length
Lyman 5A	2/29 to 1934	5X	3/4″	16″
438 Field	1930 to 1947	3X, 4X	3/4″	17″
#22 Jr. Field	1935 to 1936	2 1/2X	3/4″	12 1/2″
#422 Expert	1936 to 1942	4X	3/4″	13 1/2″
Jr. Targetspot	1937 to 1957	6X, 8X, 10X	3/4″	21 1/4″
Targetspot	1935 to 1948	8X, 10X	3/4″	22″
Super Targetspot	1937 to 1978	10X, 12X, 15X, 20X, 25X, 30X	3/4″	24 3/8″

WILLIAM MALCOLM

On pages 126 through 129, Dr. Franklin W. Mann in *The Bullet's Flight* describes, in detail, a telescopic mount for mounting a telescope on a rifle. In an examination of this mount, the observer will immediately notice the similarity to the mounts made by Wm. Malcolm, the telescope maker, who was active from the 1840's until 1890.

Although it is not generally known, telescopic sights were mounted on sniper rifles and used during the Civil War. Many of these telescopes were made by William Malcolm who was born

October 13, 1823 and died July 12, 1890. His shop was located at Syracuse, New York.

The work of the Malcolm Rifle Telescope Company was carried on by others after his death. The company was relocated in Auburn, New York and continued in business until after World War II.

The No. 1 scope was the best as far as resolution was concerned. As for the mountings, the tube was grooved similarly to the Lyman 5A to enable the telescope to recoil in a straight line.

The Malcolm "C" mounts were clamped to the tubes and did not permit the tube to slide. The front mount ring was fixed to a cross slide which provided the windage with the adjustment being made by screws on either side of the mount. To correct for windage, move the scope in the opposite direction from the direction we are used to at the present time.

The rear mount has a yoke arrangement in which a square collar slides for elevation. The divisions on the elevation wheel are in 12's, and each mark represents 1 inch at 100 yards when the mounts are spaced 7.2 inches apart. These mounts dovetail into the barrel, although some had standard bases fixed to the mounts which were screwed directly to the barrel. Some later ones were grooved for target bases which were narrower and lower than standard bases.

Malcolm telescopes were all made with ¾" tubes without an enlarged eyepiece or objective lens. The telescopes were made in 14", 16", 18" and 20" lengths in 1932. Earlier telescopes were made in 24" to 32" lengths.

The No. 1 model could be obtained in various magnifications from 4X to 10X. The No. 4 was made in 4X, 6X and 8X magnifications.

The field of view at 100 yards was as follows: 4X, 25.5 feet; 6X, 18 feet; 8X, 13.5 feet. Because of the narrow field of view, the telescopes were only practical for target or stationary objects.

The reticules were in three choices; cross-hairs; aiming post; cross-hairs with dot in the center. The cross-hairs were very fine. The eye relief was 1 ¾"; a 2 ½" eye relief could be had upon special order. The longer eye relief reduced the small field of view even further.

The tube metal was thin but rugged. The parallax adjustment was simple; a plate at the front part held by a small screw could be adjusted for focus. A short plate with screw near the ocular end could be moved to clear up the reticule and to remove the parallax.

The ends of the telescopes were protected by metal threaded caps.

Telescopes in 2½X and 3X were recommended for hunting. These telescopes were universal focus with a field of view at 100 yards of 45 feet and 34 feet respectively.

The Malcolm telescopes were well made and reasonable in price, but they could not be compared with fine target telescopes like the Fecker, Lyman, and Unertl telescopes made at a later date.

STEVENS ARMS AND TOOL COMPANY

The target telescopes used by the shooters of single shot rifles in the early days were mainly Malcolm, Stevens, and Winchester. The most important of the telescope makers was the J. Stevens Arms & Tool Company. In my Book *100 Years of Shooters and Gunmakers of Single Shot Rifles,* I charted all the various models of the Stevens line.

Prior to 1901 the Stevens rifles were sold with telescopes furnished by the Cataract Tool & Optical Company of Buffalo, New York. In 1901 Stevens purchased the Optical Company and the services of their superintendent, F. L. Smith. Smith redesigned the telescopes, and for the first time the eye piece lens system was incorporated in a slide in the tube about seven inches long. Many of the cheaper telescopes of the 1930's later followed this same procedure to the extent that many of them are actually interchangeable.

The Stevens telescopes were universal focus with just minor adjustments available in a slight slide and screw arrangement. The optical system was made of high quality optical glass.

The "Favorite" was the first low priced quality telescope manufactured with target type mounts and fine adjustments.

The #350 26 inch scope sold for $8.00 and was 4x magnification. The #355 was 6X. The #360 was 28 inches long, was 8X and sold for $10.00.

The "Ideal" telescopes were made with aplanatic eyepieces and achromatic objective lenses.

The "Acme Telescope" was the finest of the Stevens line.

In 1903 Stevens further expanded their telescope line, and "Favorite" was manufactured in tube lengths from 26 inches to 32. Longer lengths could be obtained on special order.

Again in 1907 a number of major improvements had been added to the line.

The mounts offered were based on the original Pope suggested mounts, using micrometer type adjustments. The early mounts were dovetailed into the barrel of the rifle. Later the mounts had solid bases attached to the barrel with the well-known two screw arrangement. Still later the mounts became the typical dovetail mounts which could be removed from the bases and replaced with a minimum effort.

Stevens' pioneering work in the way of mounts became the standard for later manufacturers to follow, and the base hole spacing became the standard for the industry which is still true today.

Stevens telescope mounts. The one on the left is an early mount with screw adjustment and dovetailed into the barrel. The one on the right has micrometer adjusting screws. The mount is on a fixed base which is mounted on the barrel with screws.

J. W. SIDLE

John Sidle was born in 1847 and died December 23, 1918. Mr. Sidle made very fine telescopes which were used by many shooters during the Schuetzen days.

When Harry M. Pope returned to the East from his disastrous experience in the San Francisco earthquake, J. W. Sidle, the rifle telescope maker who was located on 12th Street in Philadelphia, Pennsylvania, gave him a job.

Pope worked for Sidle until Sidle decided to move his business to Corning, California. In 1908 Pope went into business for himself in Jersey City, New Jersey. Sidle continued to make telescopes for riflemen at his Corning, California place of business.

FRED L. SMITH

Mr. Smith was associated with the Stevens Firearms Company as superintendent of the rifle telescope department. Later, he was replaced by his son, Wells.

From 1913 to 1918 he made rifle telescopes for H. M. Pope as well as others under his own name. Mr. Smith's last shop was located at 588 Dickenson Street, Springfield, Massachusetts.

One of the best known Smith telescopes was the one which H. M. Pope had Mr. Smith make for C. W. Rowland. This telescope had parallax in it when it was sent to Mr. Rowland. Since Mr. Rowland did not have the knowledge necessary to correct the fault, the telescope became well known. Later Pope and others were able to explain how parallax is corrected, and the Smith telescope became one of Mr. Rowland's favorites.

I have found some of today's rifle telescopes, which shooters are attempting to use, to have unadjusted parallax. Telescopes used for big game hunting do not have parallax adjustment since the amount is so small as to have no practical importance.

Target telescopes of 10X or above do need parallax adjustment. If you adjust for zero parallax at 100 yards, then near or far distances beyond that point will not be in focus if we use a camera term.

In hunting telescopes, if the reticule is not mounted precisely at the correct distance from the objective lens, parallax will occur at all ranges, and the telescope appears to be out of focus. Most hunting telescopes are adjusted for 100 yards.

In addition to parallax, there is also the necessity of adjusting the eyepiece for proper focus for your eye. In my own case, people who look through my telescopes say that everything looks "fuzzy" but to my eye they are sharp and that's where I want it. The viewed object and the reticule must be in a clear relationship when viewed by the shooter. You cannot have someone else adjust your telescope and expect to get a clear focus; it is something that you must learn to do for yourself.

Since changing a telescope from one rifle to another will change the point of impact of the bullet, be sure to keep a notebook with the information about the telescope, its sight setting for each rifle, as well as the individual rifle range settings. This includes yardage adjustment, windage, and elevation, as well as cartridge loading for that particular range.

WINCHESTER REPEATING ARMS COMPANY

On February 9, 1909 Winchester received a patent for a top mounted rifle telescope with target adjustments and sliding bases which permitted the removal of the sight from the gun and its re-installation. The rear adjustable mount has a distinctive spring inserted in the mount which rests against the telescope to keep the scope tube firmly held in the mount.

Some shooters find fault with the Winchester target telescope, but other shooters who have used these scopes for many years still find them reliable instruments. This speaks well for the Winchester target telescope.

The sight was made in two styles and three powers. The style A5 had the largest field and best illumination. The A-5 designated the model number and the power of the glass. The A model was made in 3X and 5X power. The Winchester catalogs mention the A in only 5X power; however, I recently examined a Winchester telescope clearly marked A3, so it was made. The B model numbers were B5, B4, and B3; the numbers designate the power of the telescope.

The eye relief, that is the distance from the eyepiece of the telescope to the eye, for style A was 2 inches and for style B 3 ½ inches. Both the ocular and objective lenses were adjustable. This was the rifle telescope that had a lens system adjustable within the telescope itself.

The reticule was offered in cross-hairs, triangle, aperture, and a pin head. The choice of a reticule was dependent upon the buyer's decision.

The mounts themselves were made of nickel steel. The adjustments of the mounts permitted shooting at ranges up to 500 yards. The rear mounts were offered in No. 1 and No. 2 size. The no. 1 micrometer readings were in .003 of an inch. The No. 2 mount was in .001 of an inch. The division marks on both the adjusting screws and the mounts were in red enamel.

The tube of this telescope was bored and drilled from a solid piece of steel. One of the accessories which was available with this scope was an offset base adapter to permit the telescope to set off to the left from the normal mountings.

The Winchester telescope rights were later purchased by the Lyman Gun Sight Company.

WOLLENSAK

The Wollensak target rifle telescope was a ¾ inch tube type measuring 15 ¾ inches long. It was made in 4 power and had a 23 foot field of view at 100 yards. The eye relief was 2 inches, and the weight of the complete telescope and mounts was 17 ounces.

These telescopes were popular for low priced target use during the 1930's and were top mounted using the regular dovetail scope blocks mounted on the barrel.

This telescope was made by the Wollensack Optical Company of Rochester, New York.

The mounts for the Wollensak telescope, like the Marlin and Mossberg telescopes, were made of cast white metal.

These telescopes are occasionally found on .25 caliber single shot rifles as well as on .22's. I have found them on .32's occasionally.

These low cost telescopes were popular during the 1930's and 1940's and served a need. They were capable of producing some very fine scores.

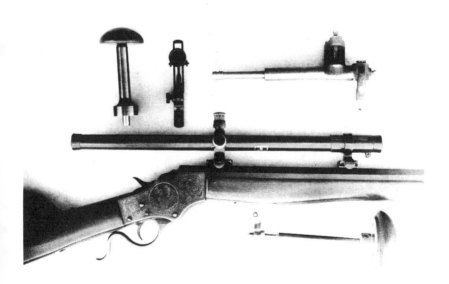

Wollensak target telescope with sliding mounts to absorb the recoil on a Stevens .32-40 model 44 1/2 action with a number 5 barrel. Pope type bullet starter, Stevens-Pope lubricating pump. Threaded adjustable palmrest. Stevens tang sight.

O. F. MOSSBERG AND SONS, INC.

Oscar F. Mossberg came to this country in 1886. He was employed by the Iver Johnson Company where he demonstrated his mechanical ingenuity in the development of firearms. Later, he worked for the Shattuck Arms Co. of Hatfield, Massachusetts. From 1900 to 1914 he worked for the J. Stevens Arms Company at Chicopee Falls, Massachusettes. 1914-1919 he was employed by the Marlin-Rockwell corporation who had taken over the old Marlin Arms Company.

In 1919 he formed his own company and began the manufacture of a low cost quality firearm line.

Although late for the peak of the single shot rifle Schuetzen type of competition, they did supply a low cost quality sight used by shooters during the 1930's and 1940's.

The first rifle telescope in the Mossberg line was offered by 1934 as the Model #6. This telescope had a universal type mount with accurate external adjustments in the front mount. This was a 4 power scope and cross-hairs were standard, although a post could be supplied on special order.

In 1936, the 8A telescope was introduced in 4 power.

In 1937, there were four Model 6 telescope sights listed. These telescopes measured 15 ⅜ inches in length and weighed 20 ounces complete.

No. 6c was a model 6 with micrometer click adjustments in 4 power.

No. L6C was the same except it was made for a left hand bolt action.

No. 6E8 had micrometer click adjustment and was a combination telescope with 4 and 8 power in the same unit.

No. L6E8 was the same except for a left hand bolt action.

No. 8A was 1 ½ power with a wider field of view than the number 6.

No. L8A again was the same as the 8A but for left hand action guns.

The Model 8's were 13 inches in length and weighed 15 ounces complete.

The conventional micrometer adjustable mountings with dovetail mounts and bases were not offered until 1937. This latter development permitted the telescope to be used on any rifle which had the traditional dovetail bases which had been developed by Stevens, Winchester, Lyman, and others.

7C telescopes were 15⅜ inches long with a ¾ inch diameter tube, weight was 20 ounces, 4 and 8 power. This model scope, the 7C and 7C8 changed power by interchanging the eyepieces.

In 1937, the R models were introduced and these had adjustable reticules.

The "A" telescopes were variable in power from 2½ to 6 power.

In 1938, Mossberg introduced the first range finding rifle telescope.

The No. 9 telescopes also introduced in 1938 involved changes in the mount system with the introduction of a side mount plate.

The telescopes used by the single shot shooters were primarily the No. 7 series with their precision click type micrometer one-half minute of angle adjustments. The mounts were made for the traditional dovetail target base mounted on the barrel. Included with the bases were brass shims which could be inserted under the block to get the adjustment needed. Except for the Pope and Niedner bases which were machined to fit the barrel, most of the regularly manufactured bases did require some shimming for a good fit. Most of these shims I have found were made of shellacked cardboard, although brass shims are also found.

The Mossberg #7 was 4X and had a cross-hair reticule. Because the bases were standard, the telescope could be used with

Three different types adjustable target mounts used on Mossberg rifle telescopes.

Lyman, Fecker, Marlin, or Wollensak target scope bases. The tube was ¾" with a ⅝" objective lens; the length of the tube was 15 ⅞".

Mossberg also made variable power telescopes which were introduced to the shooting public in 1937. The Mossberg spotting scope used on the target ranges was first announced in 1935.

JOHN UNERTL

John Unertl, Sr. learned the fundamentals of optical sights during service in the German army. In 1928 he, his wife Anna, and son John Unertl, Jr. emigrated to the United States via Argentina.

His first employment in the U. S. was with the J. W. Fecker telescope manufacturing company located at Pittsburgh, Pennsylvania. Later Unertl became the superintendent of the Fecker plant.

One of the workmen who worked for him was Wray Hageman. Hageman was to later leave the Fecker company and become the designer for the telescope manufacturing division of the Lyman Gun Sight Company. It was his efforts which led eventually to the excellent telescopes produced by Lyman.

In 1936 Unertl decided to leave Fecker and start his own business. At first the company operated out of the basement of his new home. The entire staff consisted of John, Sr., his wife Anna, and son John, Jr. John, Jr. became the designer of the rifle telescope line. The lenses were ground, as they still are, by the Unertl Company. The rifle telescopes have always been known for their high quality and excellent workmanship. Today, the John Unertl Company is one of the last companies in the United States to produce the external adjustment target rifle telescopes.

When the company first started, the dovetailed micrometer adjustable telescope mounts were furnished by the J. W. Fecker Optical Company. Later these mounts were supplied by the Lyman Gun Sight Company. Today, as has been true in the immediate past, the mounts are manufactured by the Unertl Company itself.

One type of sight manufactured by both Lyman and Unertl was known as a tube sight. This sight which has the appearance of a telescope has no optical lens system; it does have an adjustable peep which regulates the amount of light on the sight and target. The tube is used in conjunction with an iron target front sight. Shooters found these to be excellent sights for indoor shooting, but presented problems when used on outdoor ranges. Because the tube sight required an adjustment at the front to keep it parallel, some shooters replaced the front mount with a rear mount, making the tube double adjustable. This double adjustable feature was only necessary when shooting outdoors and at 100 yards or more.

UNERTL TARGET TELESCOPES

Model	Power	Length	Tube Diameter	Eyepiece Diameter	Objective Diameter
1"	6X, 8X, 10X	21 1/2"	3/4"	7/8"	1"
1 1/4"	8X, 10X 12X, 14X	24"	3/4"	7/8"	1 1/4"
1 1/2"	10X, 12X 16X, 18X, 20X	25 1/2"	3/4"	7/8"	1 1/2"
2"	10X, 15X 18X, 20X 24X	24"	1"	1 1/8"	1 1/2"
Small Game	3X, 4X 6X	18"	3/4"	3/4"	3/4"

Today the rifle telescope division of the Unertl Company is only one small part of the company. The service offered the shooters, however, is in the old tradition and with quality workmanship an assured part of that tradition.

J. W. FECKER TELESCOPES

The J. W. Fecker Company was located at Pittsburgh, Pennsylvania and produced quality target telescopes for rifles. The target mounts had ¼ minute clicks. A lower cost mount had ½ minute adjustments but was not very popular.

The telescopes were made from 4½ power to 10 power in the ¾ inch tube which was 20 inches long and weighed 15 ounces complete.

The big telescope with a 1 ⅛ inch objective was made in 6 to 12 ½ power and was 22 inches long with a total weight of 17 ounces.

Although the Fecker telescopes were popular with the target shooters, they were made long after the height of the Schuetzen shooting and were not used by the early shooters. They may be found on single shot rifles today for they are excellent range scopes.

By 1932 the J. W. Fecker Company, located at 2016 Perrysville Ave., Pittsburgh, Pennsylvania, was advertising their new and improved 1 ⅛″ and 1 ½″ objectives which could be added to the old ¾″ tube telescopes originally made by the Fecker Company.

Some of the older Fecker telescopes found today will have these objectives added.

LITSCHERT TARGET TELESCOPES

R. A. Litschert of Winchester, Indiana began his optical business by specializing in making optical converters which converted regular low power hunting telescopes to target or varmint telescopes.

These converters were 8X and could be screwed on to the front of an existing telescope for which it was made. The converters had coated optics and provision for focusing for different ranges. These converters proved very practical.

Later, after World War II, Litschert began making regular target telescopes. By 1960 the Litschert Company manufactured the following:

Model	Magnification Power	Length of Tube
Spot Shot 1 1/4"	10X, 12X 15X, 20X	25"
Spot Shot 1 1/2"	10X, 12X, 15X	25"
	20X, 25X, 30X	27"

The Litschert telescopes were very well made and of high quality. These scopes were used in target shooting and in bench rest shooting. The mounts were of the conventional adjustable dovetail type mounts.

The Litschert rifle telescope will still be found on many range rifles.

The optics were coated and the click adjustments were in one fourth inch at 100 yards. The objective adjustment slides in a screw slot rather than by turning a threaded section.

Mr. Litschert retired and the telescope business was taken over by Myron Davis who operates under the name of Davis Optical Co. at Winchester, Indiana.

JOHN JAMIESON AND JOHN REDFIELD
DENVER, COLORADO

John Jamieson of Denver, Colorado, was born in Colorado in 1893 and was a shooter all his life. Like others who were skilled gunsmiths, he made a target telescope very similar in appearance to the Stevens telescopes of the early 1900's.

The Jamieson telescopes were made in two styles. One was the target type of Stevens with a ¾ tube and the other a rugged hunting scope with a ⅞" tube and enlarged objective.

The ¾" tubes were 16 inches long in 4X. The mounts used were Lyman, Mossberg or similar types. The tubes were browned, not blued. About 12 of these scopes are known to have been made - there is no name or identifying mark on the scope.

The hunting telescopes used a Malcolm early type mount but manufactured by Jamieson. Again, no marks appear on the telescopes.

Other little known makers like Jamieson made target telescopes for individual target shooters. Some of the telescopes show a very high degree of skill.

Mr. Jamieson made very fine windgauge front sights in the Winchester, Remington, and Sharps pattern. These sights show very high quality workmanship. His rear sights were finely made tang sights made to fit Ballards, Sharps, and other single shot rifles.

The single shot target rifles were his life long interest and he made a number of very fine Schuetzen rifles.

Mr. Jamieson also made set triggers for Ballard rifles which were similar to the factory sets.

I know of one rifle action he made which is, to all appearances, a Farrow, but has some minor variation from the Farrow.

Some of Mr. Jamieson's ideas were incorporated in the sights made by the Western Gun Sight Company operated by John Redfield at Denver, Colorado. Mr. Redfield also experimented with single shot rifles. One of his developments was a hammerless Ballard action.

John Redfield was born on a homesteaded ranch near Glendale, Oregon in 1859. He roamed the west, working wherever and whenever his fancy took him. For a time he ran a bicycle shop in Medford, Oregon, but in the early 1900's John and his brother Edward headed for Denver, Colorado and the mining country.

In July of 1909 John decided to start a company manufacturing gun sights in a small building at 3315 Gilpin Street in Denver. Although John established the business, Edward continued to work in the shop on his own and perfected the rifle which became known as the Stevens .22 Visible-Loading Rifle. Edward received a royalty on each rifle Stevens produced. He died in 1917.

The company was at first called the Western Gunsight Company, but the Western Cartridge Company claimed a trademark infringement, so the name was changed to the Redfield Gun Sight Comapny.

One of John Redfield's sights was known as the Sourdough Patridge. This sight was well liked, but it led to a court suit which was decided in Redfield's favor and the sight continued to be made.

John was joined by his son Watt, and later, about 1934, by a Owen Fytegraff who became a third partner. John died in 1943. The company continued in business under the same partnership

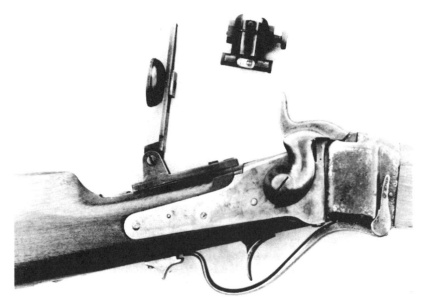

John Jamieson, Denver, Colo. Sharps windgauge spirit level front sight and Sharps rear tang sight with folding leaf on Sharps 1874 .45-100.

arrangement. In 1957 the partnership again became a threesome with the name of Ed Hilliard added.

By 1965 the Redfield Company produced one thousand different sighting products. During the development period and depending upon the contract, many Winchester and Remington rifles used Redfield sights as part of their standard equipment.

The original Stith Sight Company had been bought out by the Kollmorgan Optical Company of North Hampton, Massachusetts. Kollmorgan in turn was bought by the Redfield Company and added to their optical sight production.

Today quality optical sights are still produced by the company in the tradition of John Redfield, the original founder.

John Jamieson, Denver, Colo., rifle telescope and a tang target sight.

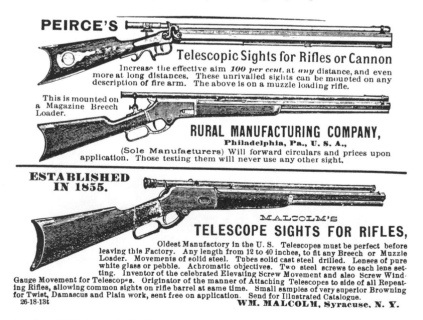

PEIRCE'S

Telescopic Sights for Rifles or Cannon

Increase the effective aim *100 per cent.* at *any* distance, and even more at long distances. These unrivalled sights can be mounted on any description of fire arm. The above is on a muzzle loading rifle.

This is mounted on a Magazine Breech Loader.

RURAL MANUFACTURING COMPANY,
Philadelphia, Pa., U. S. A.,

(Sole Manufacturers) Will forward circulars and prices upon application. Those testing them will never use any other sight.

ESTABLISHED IN 1855.

MALCOLM'S
TELESCOPE SIGHTS FOR RIFLES,

Oldest Manufactory in the U. S. Telescopes must be perfect before leaving this Factory. Any length from 12 to 40 inches, to fit any Breech or Muzzle Loader. Movements of solid steel. Tubes solid cast steel drilled. Lenses of pure white glass or pebble. Achromatic objectives. Two steel screws to each lens setting. Inventor of the celebrated Elevating Screw Movement and also Screw Wind-Gauge Movement for Telescopes. Originator of the manner of Attaching Telescopes to side of all Repeating Rifles, allowing common sights on rifle barrel at same time. Small samples of very superior Browning for Twist, Damascus and Plain work, sent free on application. Send for Illustrated Catalogue.
26-18-13t   **WM. MALCOLM, Syracuse, N. Y.**

American Field, Page vi, October 30, 1886.

CHAPTER 6

COMMERCIALLY PRODUCED SIGHTS AND RELOADING TOOLS

BULLARD REPEATING ARMS COMPANY

J. H. Bullard, the inventor of the Bullard rifle system, was the master mechanic for the Smith and Wesson Revolver Company for many years.

The Bullard Arms Association was organized in 1882 and reorganized in 1883 as the Bullard Repeating Arms Company.

The actual manufacturing of the rifles began in 1884. The first single shot rifles were advertised in 1885. The rifles were well made and of quality parts. Many of the Bullard cartridges were modified from other rifle cartridges of that period.

Reloading tools were developed by the Bullard Arms Company for cartridges to be used in their rifles. The reloading tools were simple in-line hand tools as shown in their catalog.

Note that the illustrations in the catalog of the sights available for the Bullard rifles indicate that the sights are made by the Lyman Gunsight Company and the Winchester Repeating Arms Company, and are the standard production sights.

28   BULLARD REPEATING ARMS COMPANY.   SPRINGFIELD, MASS., U. S. A.

Price List of Cartridges for Hunting Rifles.

Cartridges for all our arms are manufactured by the U. M. C. Co., and are guaranteed to be of first quality. Solid head and re-loadable shells.

	40 grains Powder,	150 Grains lead, $31.50 per M.	Shells, $20	Bullets, $7.25 per M.
32 Cal	40 grains Powder	150 Grains lead, $31.50 per M.	$20	$7.25 per M.
38 Cal	45 "	190 " 31.50 "	" 20	" 8.00 "
40 Cal	45 "	258 " 33.00 "	" 18	" 9.00 "
40 Cal	75 "	300 " 40.00 "	" 22	" 10.50 "
45 Cal	90 "	300 " 33.00 "	" 20	" 9.00 "
45 Cal	60 "	350 " 35.00 "	" 20	" 9.50 "
45 Cal	75 "	405 " 35.00 "	" 22	" 12.00 "
45 Cal	70 "	290 " 37.00 "	" 22	" 9.50 "
50 Cal	85 "	300 " 40.00 "	" 23	" 11.00 "
50 Cal	95 "	300 " Exp. " 90.00 "	" 50	" 11.00 "
50 Cal	115 "	346 " 90.00 "	" 50	" 9.00 "

Primers $2 per M.

Directions for Re-loading Cartridges with the Bullard Re-loader.

To prepare the shell. Wash the fired shells in strong soap suds or soda water, and dry thoroughly. Place the fired shell in sizing die. Place sizing die and shell in anvil with the shallow cup upward. Strike the sizing die until the shell is forced completely in. Turn over anvil, put plunger into the shell, which will extract shell from the sizing die and expel the exploded primer.

Now put this reduced shell into the loader with the head end up. Put on the primers and seat with the primer seater. Remove the shell, fill with powder, well shaken down, preferably loaded through a tube, so that the powder shall be even full in the shell. Place the ball evenly on the shell, with the shell in the anvil, shallow cup upward. Place over the crimper and drive down to the shoulder, preferably with a wooden mallet.

Great care should be used in preparing cartridges of an even length and in every case the crimper should be driven down to the shoulder.

We will guarantee our rifles in every case when the cartridges are re-loaded with the above tools, according to these directions.

Primer Seater.

Plunger.

Anvil.   Sizing Die.

Loader and Crimper.

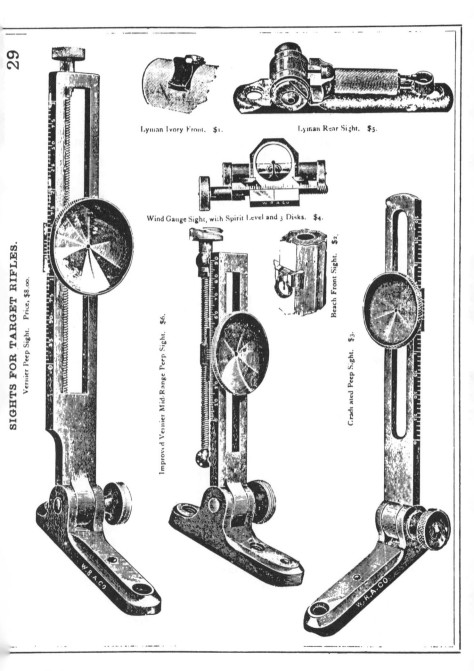

29

SIGHTS FOR TARGET RIFLES.

Vernier Peep Sight.   Price, $8.00.

Lyman Ivory Front. $1.

Lyman Rear Sight. $5.

Wind Gauge Sight, with Spirit Level and 3 Disks. $4.

Improved Vernier Mid-Range Peep Sight. $6.

Beach Front Sight. $2.

Graduated Peep Sight. $3.

Bullard Arms Co., Springfield, Mass. Catalog, 1887-1888.

LYMAN GUNSIGHT CORPORATION

Although the name Lyman and Ideal have become synonymous, one must remember that Lyman's takeover of the Ideal Company did not take place until October, 1925.

Lyman was a strong supporter of the Ideal tools from the very beginning and supported the Ideal Handbook series with its advertising.

The Lyman Company began back in 1878 and began its life as a one man company making sights for the shooting fraternity. The founder was William Lyman, born in 1854 and who died in 1896.

The company, under the leadership of William Lyman and later other members of the Lyman family, catered to the desires of the hunters and target shooters. The product which was furnished was of the best material and workmanship. In fact, in my opinion, the old Lyman company was the leader in the entire field of sights and provided a high standard for all, including the arms companies as well as the individual makers.

Because of the high quality and manufacturing standards, old established arms companies turned in increasing numbers to the Lyman Company for their sighting equipment.

The Ideal #7 Handbook had illustrations of the Lyman gun sights, one of which was the Beach front sight, patented August 31, 1880.

Others advertised were the No. 1 tang combination sight patented May 6, 1884, the ivory bead #18 windgauge sight patented January 28, 1891, the #17 front target sight, the #7 globe windgauge front sight patented January 8, 1889, as well as the #8 Beach windgauge sight patented July 14, 1891.

As previously mentioned, the Lyman tang sight No. 15, patented August 23, 1887, was the first successful adjustable tang sight produced. The sight was adjustable both for windage and elevation.

A later No. 2 combination rear tang sight proved to be very popular and was used by many target shooters although there was no windage adjustment in the base.

The #29 tang sight was another good sight with both elevation and windgauge adjustment. This sight was patented March 6, 1900, but had disappeared from the Lyman listings by 1903. The windage adjustment was not made by a knob, but rather by a hinged flat turn wedge.

Later a No. 103 rear tang sight was offered. This sight was

finely made and was micrometer adjustable for both elevation and windage.

One tang sight that is often miscalled a "Pope" sight was the No. 47 Lyman tang sight which was adjustable for elevation. The target top was known as the No. 52a and had a small machined steel square which contained the windage adjustment made by a small knurled knob in one quarter turn increments. This sight often appears on the late .22 rimfire High Wall Winchester Schuetzen rifles.

Two different Lyman #103 rear tang sights. These sights have both windguage and adjustments and no longer made the windgauge front sight necessary.

From 1885 *American Field*

Lyman rifle sights a windgauge front sight with spirit level, two #103 windage and elevation adjustment tang sights, and four tang sights with elevation only.

MARLIN FIREARMS COMPANY

Originally, J. M. Marlin entered the firearms field as a manufacturer of pistols. Marlin began the manufacture of rifles based on the Ballard patent rights with the assistance of Daly of Schoverling and Daly, New York City, who had purchased the patent rights to the Ballard rifle in 1873. The Ballard rifles had reloading tools furnished as accessories.

The re- and de-primer tools are well finished, flat hinged pliers type devices with the de-capping leg on one side and the flat rounded handle re-primer on the other side. The de-capping pin is covered by an acorn designed knurled screw-on cap.

The bullet seating chamber is a finely finished, flared base, hand held tool with a separate palm plunger marked with the caliber of the tool.

The case was de-primed and re-primed with the hinged tool, then the case was charged with powder, and the bullet was started into the case by hand. The case and bullet were then inserted in the hand chamber, and the plunger was seated in the tool. The base of the chamber was placed on a firm surface and the plunger was forced down with palm pressure until seated firmly on the top of the hand chamber. This completed the cartridge, ready for firing.

Early Ballards used paper patched bullets with a card wad over the powder, a thick lubricating disc, and then another card wad, sometimes sealed with a thin shellac, and the patched bullet seated over this.

Some early bullet molds with iron handles look identical to the Winchester molds but have a M.F.A. Co. stamp on them. These molds apparently were made by Winchester for Marlin.

The Ideal molds which are found with early Marlin tools are marked only with the Ideal name.

The Ballard reloading tools were still being offered for sale as late as 1898, and it is probable that some were in unsold dealer stocks for some years afterwords.

John Browning patented a plier type reloading tool complete with attached mold October 4, 1881. This tool was manufactured by the Marlin Firearms Company and is marked M.F.A. Co. with the caliber of the tool.

On May 16, 1910 the Marlin Firearms Company took over the Ideal Manufacturing Company, and the Ideal tools bear the name of the Marlin Firearms Co. during the period the company owned the Ideal Company.

Ballard sights were manufactured by Marlin and, in some instances, other firearms companies used the same sights, also apparently furnished by Marlin.

The Marlin Firearms Company, like Mossberg and Wollensak, produced a low priced target telescope in the 1930's and 1940's.

The target telescopes were top mounted ¾ inch tubes utilizing a click micrometer external adjustment mounted on standard dovetail barrel mounted bases. The length of the tube was 15½ inches. The telescopes were 4 power. The No. 1 telescope had ½ minute clicks in the rear mount, whereas the No. 2 had ½ minute of angle clicks. The bases furnished for these telescopes were case hardened.

Because of the similarity, it is believed that the "Ranger" target scope with cast white metal micrometer adjustment mounts was made by Marlin. This telescope was well made and low in cost. It was introduced through Sears Roebuck and Company about 1937-38 and was the first of many telescopes. The tube was brass, ¾″ in diameter, and was about 15 inches long. The scope used the eye piece lens system developed by Smith for Stevens in 1901. The tube had end retaining rings which were threaded on the tube.

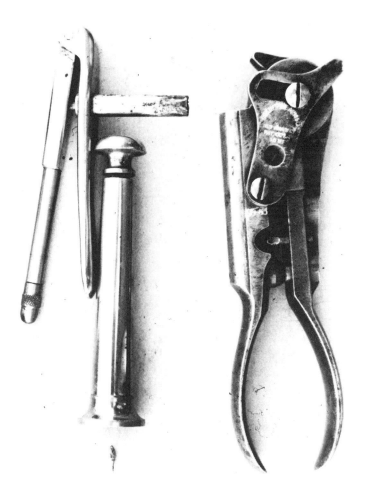

Set of Marlin Firearms Co. reloading tools. The tool on the right was patented in 1881 by J. M. Browning of Ogden, Utah, and has a mold, re and de capper, bullet seating chamber all within the tool. Lower is a Ballard straight line bullet seating chamber and a re- and de-capper. Ideal molds as well as Marlin Firearms Co. molds were used to cast the bullets for this set. Some Bridgeport Gun Implement molds were used. These look the same as later Sharps molds.

MAYNARD, MASSACHUSETTS ARMS COMPANY

The Maynard rifle and tools were made at Chicopee Falls, Massachusetts by the Massachusetts Arms Company.

The reloading tool of 1882 was a very simple device which consisted of a de-capping pin to remove the fired primer from the cartridge case, a plunger type smooth seater die and a round anvil to set the case rim in. A wad cutter was also furnished.

During the time the Berdan primers were used, a small handle device was used to prick the primer and remove it in one smooth operation. This device was patented by Hadley, March 26, 1878.

The bullet was seated by inserting the bullet into the charged case with the fingers, then putting the cartridge into the smooth

Reloading tools with an 1882 cased Maynard rifle set. The set consists of a Hadley re- and de-capper, a mold, a wad cutter, a straight line bullet seater, base and cartridge case. Collection of Jack L. Houchen, Colo.

bodied seating chamber, inserting the whole into the anvil or base, and pushing down to the seat the bullet.

The illustrations shown here are from the 1880 catalog.

Sights for Maynard Rifles.

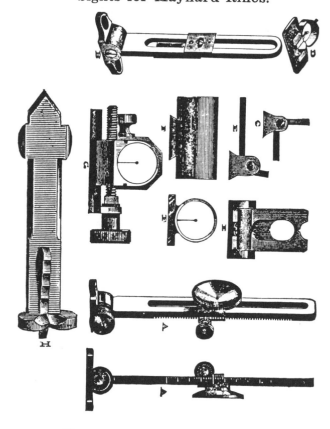

The New Patent Attachment,

For using rim or central fire fixed ammunition,—patented Oct. 5, 1880.

The invention of this attachment answers the objections made by some parties that fixed ammunition could not be used with the Maynard rifle. By the use of this attachment "The Maynard" uses a greater variety of ammunition than any other gun manufactured. It is attached to the breech-piece by means of two small screws, easily removed.

The length, calibre and prices of barrels especially manufactured to be used with this Attachment can be found on a page in this catalogue under the heading "Prices of Barrels."

Reproduction of page from 1880 Mass. Arms Co. catalog.

The Maynard Improved Cartridge.

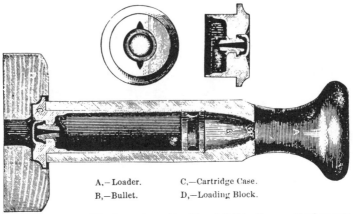

A,—Loader. C,—Cartridge Case.
B,—Bullet. D,—Loading Block.

An inspection of the foregoing cut will exhibit to the practical sportsman some of the peculiar advantages of the Maynard arms.

The cartridges are loaded with an implement like a starter, which secures placing the bullet with mathematical precision, where it remains in the same position through the barrel until delivered. The position of the primer and bullet renders the cartridges perfectly water-proof. The slot—Parker's patent—as shown in the head of the cartridge, enables the cap to be removed after the discharge, with perfect ease. The quality of powder is subject to the sportsman's own selection, and the expense for ammunition is covered by the bare cost of powder, lead and primers, as the cartridge cases are susceptible of reloading for an indefinite number of times. (See directions for loading, on next page.)

Calibre of Cartridges for Rifles and Shot Guns.

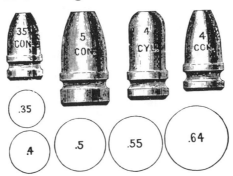

Reproduction of page from 1880 Mass. Arms Co. catalog.

STEVENS ARMS COMPANY

By 1901, the Stevens Firearms Company of Chicopee Falls, Massachusetts, was considered to be one of the foremost manufacturers of fine target rifles.

The smooth working Model 44 rifle action was introduced by Stevens in 1894; the introduction of the improved action in the 1904 catalog known as the 44 ½ established Stevens in the target rifle field.

As a result of the merger of Harry M. Pope with the Stevens Firearms Company in 1901, the Stevens Company gained the Pope line of Schuetzen loading tools as well as the expertise to manufacture them.

The tool offered by Stevens was the Pope "Loading Flask" which was a powder measure throwing a double powder charge of smokeless powder primer and the main charge of black powder.

Pope had been making these powder measures for shooters who had purchased his rifles. The only difference between the regular Pope measure and the Stevens model is in the finish.

Next would be the molds offered by Stevens. These molds were the same type manufactured by Pope. The mold blocks were the basic Ideal Manufacturing Company blocks and handles. The mold itself was cut with the Pope type "cherries" or milling cutters to the shape of the particular bullet. The mold was modified with a double cut off plate and the bullet was cast from the point. This type of casting gives less distortion to the base of the bullet. In shooting with lead bullets, it is essential to prevent any damage to the base of the bullet. If there is even a slight damage, the shot will go out of the group and often accounts for that frustrating "flyer".

The only way to tell the difference between a Stevens-Pope mold and the regular Pope mold is in the stamped lettering. Some Pope molds are stamped with his name, but some are not. On the side of the hinge is a small drilled hole in both Pope and Stevens-Pope molds, around this hole is arranged the stamped work "WAX". In the Pope molds this lettering is smaller than that used by Stevens-Pope.

The re- and de-capper made by Stevens was the standard Pope tool. Both tools are the same and both are nickled.

The lubricating pump was made the same as the Pope and was a tool made for lubricating the special Pope shaped bullets. The die of the pump was made for a particular bullet. The screw rod, plunger rod, and bench screw were of machined steel as well as the die. The body of the pump was made of bronze. There is a slight variation in the color of the bronze, probably due to the casting made from a particular foundry operation.

On the bench clamp will frequently be found the number 187 with a P in Pope-Stevens outfits and this is presumed to be the way the Stevens product was differentiated from the regular Pope pump.

These tools were featured in the Stevens Catalog from the time Pope joined the Stevens Company through catalog #53 issued in 1911.

Although not a reloading tool, Stevens also manufactured and sold the Pope palm rest which used a sliding adjustment with a locking nut. These are the same as the regular Pope.

Stevens rifle sights varied from the plain sporting rear notch and the Rocky Mountain front blade sight to the fine windgauge front sights and the vernier windgauge tang sights with the changeable aperture sight disc.

Many of the windgauge sights were actually Lyman sights. With the plain windgauge globe front sight, a special level #14 could be used in the rear sight slot.

Stevens-made sights were used as well as the Beach combination front sight; the Lyman sight was similar to the Beach.

The Lyman tang sights used were the No. 1 and No. 2; later the No. 103 with windage and elevation were also used.

In their 1894 catalog, the Stevens Arms and Tool Company listed the regular Ideal reloading tools and equipment for their rifles. The separate bullet sizer tool, the Ideal re- and de-capper, bullet seater, and the #1 Ideal powder measure.

The 1888 Stevens Catalog featured the Malcolm telescope sights.

In 1902, the Stevens Catalog announced the purchase of the Cataract Tool and Optical Company of Buffalo, New York and that the Stevens Company would manufacture their own rifle telescopes. The mounts used on the Stevens rifle telescopes were suggested and developed by H. M. Pope while he was employed by that company. The Malcolm telescope and mount was no longer available through the Stevens Company.

After Harry M. Pope joined the Stevens Company in 1902, the Pope-Stevens Catalog featured the Pope line of molds, lubricating pumps, loading flask and re- and de-capper.

Except for the Pope tools, the Stevens company encouraged the use of Ideal reloading tools. Mr, Barlow introduced a number of tools especially adapted to the Stevens developed cartridges. To many shooters, the Stevens cartridges are unheard of calibers and sources of wonderment.

The more common Stevens calibers were prominent during the later days of the Schuetzen period from 1898 to 1908. Several of the Stevens calibers were especially popular throughout the U. S. as accurate varmint and hunting cartridges; these were the .25-20 Single Shot and the .28-30-120 which Pope particularly favored.

The terminology of the .28-30-120 is easily explained for the .28 is the caliber of the bore of the gun; 30 is the grains of black powder which the case held; and the 120 is the weight of the cast lead bullet in grains of weight.

One of the Stevens cartridges of this particular period was the slender long center fire .22-15-60; another the .25-20-86 single shot cartridge, not the same as the .25-20-86 Winchester; another the slender .25-21-86; the .25-25-86; the .28-30-120; the .32-40-165 Marlin-Winchester; and the .38-55-255 Marlin-Winchester. The .25 rim fire Stevens, both the short and the long, were also popular cartridges particularly by the squirrel hunters. I used one of those in a Remington #4 rolling block rifle and enjoyed great success with it for many years.

Opposite page — 1903-1904 Stevens Arms Co. catalog.

J. STEVENS ARMS AND TOOL COMPANY

SIGHTS – Stevens Target

Rocky Mountain Front
Sight. Price, $0.50.

No. 28.
Lyman "Semi-Jack" Front
Sight. Price, $1.00.

Open Front Sight.
Price, $0.50.

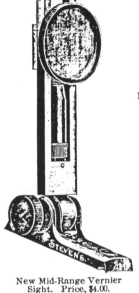

New Mid-Range Vernier
Sight. Price, $4.00.

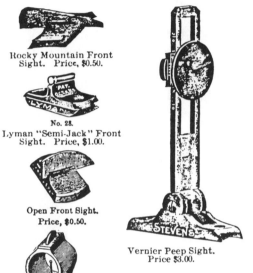

Vernier Peep Sight.
Price $3.00.

Front Sight.
Price, $1.25.

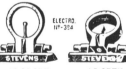

ELECTRO.
N⁹-384

AS GLOBE.   AS OPEN.
Beach Combination Front Sight.
Price, $1.00.

Front Wind Gauge Sight with Interchangeable Disc, $3. Level, $1 extra.

Open Front.
Price, $0.75.

Globe Sight with
Interchangeable Discs.
Price, $1.25.

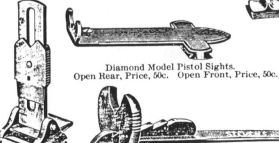

Diamond Model Pistol Sights.
Open Rear, Price, 50c.   Open Front, Price, 50c.

Rear Sight,
Price, $1.25.

Sporting Rear Sight.
Price, $0.80.. ·

E. REMINGTON AND SONS

The Remington cartridge reloading tool was a rather unusual, bulky hand tool which never attained any large degree of popularity among the shooters.

Today, this tool is rarely found, and it is a desirable collectors item.

An 1883 Remington factory catalog mentions reloading tools and gives nineteen calibers for which a grooved bullet mold was available at an extra price. The listing, as given by Remington, is not by the usual designation of bullet, powder weight, bullet weight, but one showing the caliber and the weight of the bullet. Thus, a .25-20 becomes a .25/67.

The reloading set which is offered consists of a bullet mold, seater, de-capper and re-capper, a powder measure and a wad cutter.

In listing the separate prices for the reloading implements, it gives the price of a ball seater with base. This description would only fit a hand plunger straight line seater. I have not seen a ball seater of this type which could be identified as Remington, but obviously they did exist and were used.

Remington Arms Company sights for the single shot rifles were all well made. They were sturdy sights and well machined and finished.

The line varied from the open hunting sights to the fine vernier sights of the long range rifles as shown in their catalogs. One of the most unusual sights, especially made by the Lyman Gun Sight Company for the Remington Arms Company, was that used on the light rolling block no. 7 rifle made from 1903 to 1911.

Remington "basket type" hand held reloading tool. Collection Tom Dunn, Wyo.

Shell Reducer and Expander.

NICKEL PLATED.

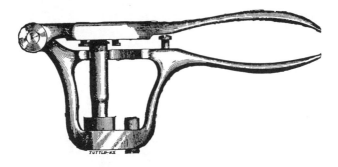

DIRECTIONS FOR USE.

After cleaning the shells thoroughly, hold the instrument in the right hand, open far enough to allow the shell to be entered sideways into its seat, catching the flange under the hook of the top piece and entering the open end of the shell into the die; then press the handles together.

This will reduce the shell at the mouth. By opening the handles the shell will be withdrawn from the die; and as it then may be a little too small it can be brought to the exact size of the bullet by the repetition of the same process, using the plug instead of the die. With new shells it will generally be sufficient to use the expanding tool only.

Always oil the shells slightly on the outside and inside of the mouth, before reducing or expanding them.

☞ We make these to fit all our solid-head rifle shells.

PRICE, $2 00

Remington reloading tool from a 1882 Remington catalog.

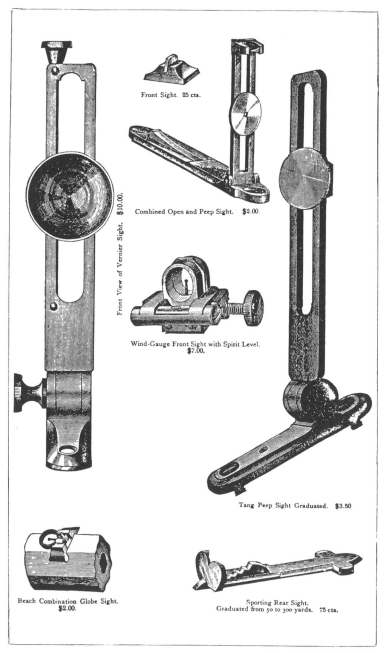

Front Sight. 25 cts.

Combined Open and Peep Sight. $2.00.

Front View of Vernier Sight, $10.00.

Wind-Gauge Front Sight with Spirit Level.
$7.00.

Tang Peep Sight Graduated. $3.50

Beach Combination Globe Sight.
$2.00.

Sporting Rear Sight.
Graduated from 50 to 300 yards.   75 cts.

Page from 1882 Remington catalog showing the rifle sights available for the Remington firearms.

U. S. MILITARY TOOLS

Frankford Arsenal made molds and reloading tools adapted to the reloading of military issue ammunition. These tools were made to encourage marksmanship programs among the troops and to lower the cost of expendable ammunition.

Today it is hard to imagine that the armed forces were ever conscious of economy. In days gone by, weapons and ammunition requirements were simple and were met by the individual training units. Today, the requirements of highly sophisticated weaponry and its use precludes the use of the weapon if its user becomes disabled and a quick replacement is needed.

It is doubtful if those who were skilled at reloading unit ammunition for target work had much of an influence on civilian reloading, but perhaps it would be well to give the information on some of the military reloading equipment.

The big gang molds which were used to cast .45/70, .45 Colt, and .30 caliber bullets were very similar to those made by the Ideal Reloading Company. At first glance they are often assumed to be one and the same thing, and only a close examination will show the U. S. Arsenal markings.

The handtools are distinctive and for the most part are assumed by the general shooter to be in the curiosity class; today's shooter can hardly imagine such tools being used.

To give the complete information in regard to the cased reloading tools issued to the individual units, the official U. S. Army Manual illustration covering this tool is shown.

The gang molds were used to cast the regular long grooved bullet as well as molds to cast a round ball used for gallery or short range practice with the regular military arms. In the black powder days the amount of powder in the case was reduced for gallery practice. Many civilians who loaded these short range cartridges put in a charge of black powder, then filled the case with "Cream of Wheat", then a thin cardboard wad over that with a disc of beeswax, and then inserted the ball by pressing it into the case mouth with the thumb.

"Candle snuffing" matches were fired at 15 feet using a round ball with only a primer in the case. If you use this idea it would be best to check the barrel after each shot to see if the bullet actually went out of the barrel. Since the striking force is greatly reduced, a backstop can usually be made of lumber or thick cardboard.

The .45/70 1873 long range rifle was made by Springfield Armory in 1879-1881. It was during this time that the Springfield Arsenal rifle team was active in the civilian shooting matches. A special case at the Springfield Arsenal Museum holds the rifles, pictures, and information concerning these shooters and their participation in the shooting at the Creedmoor Rifle Range.

Long range rifles used a Sharps rear tang sight mounted on the stock as it was on the Officer's Model of 1875. The sights were the long stem Sharps vernier sight on the tang with a standard windgauge adjustable front sight with a bubble level.

Some of these rifles used a type of rifling that varied from standard .45-70 military. The cartridge used was in some instances the .45-80-500 and in others was .45-70-500. The bullets used at first were paper patched and were purchased from the Winchester Repeating Arms Company.

The army changed from the .45-70-405 to the .45-70-500 cartridge in 1880 as it was found in shooting the long range rifles that the heavier bullet performed much better at the greater distances.

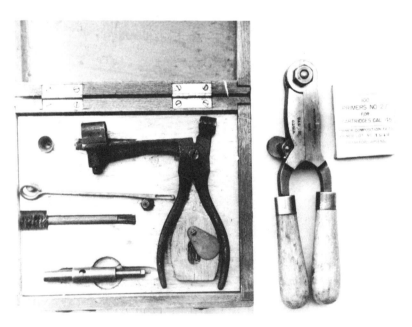

United States Frankford Arsenal cased reloading tool and armory mold for unit reloading of .30 cartridge cases. Mold - Collection Tom Dunn, Wyo.

During the course of shooting the rifles it was found that the paper patched bullets performed no better than the grooved lubricated bullets, and subsequent rifles were made for the lubricated bullet.

Less than 200 Long Range Rifles were made. In some instances these rifles are called Marksman Rifles. Some rifles were made by civilian gunsmiths and are similar to the Armory made rifles. Some of the Marksman Rifles have octagon heavy barrels and are made for cartridges other than the Army cartridge.

For further information I would suggest to the reader the book *The .45-70 Springfield* by Albert Frasca and Robert H. Hill, Springfield Publishing Company, Northridge, California, 1980.

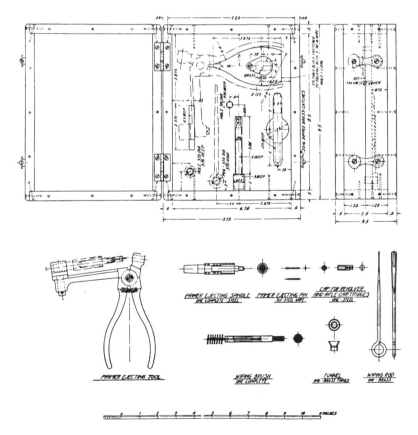

From *De-capping and Cleaning Tolls for Small-Arms Cartridges #1990* Government Printing Office, Washington D.C. 1917.

SHARPS RIFLE COMPANY

The Sharps Rifle Company from the time of its original organization as a manufacturing entity made its own sights. The company also developed its distinctive molds and unusual reloading devices.

The company continued to manufacture the mold up until the time of its final dissolution. At the time, the mold making machinery and tools were acquired by the Bridgeport Gun Implement Company. The mold was manufactured for some time as an accessory to the reloading tools offered by the B.G.I. Company to its regular trade. Some of the molds will be found marked M.F.A. These molds, while in the Sharps pattern, were made for the Marlin Firearms Company.

The distinctive Sharps mold evolved from the A. S. Nippes mold, developed for the 1849 Sharps in .52 caliber. The Nippes molds were of cast yellow brass with an iron sprue cutter.

The most familiar Sharps mold is that of the pattern of 1863, which was made for .52 caliber Civil War Cavalry Carbine. This was the government contract model, and the basic pattern of the mold remained the same throughout the life of the Sharps Rifle Company.

The bullet molds made for and used in the pistols were of a different pattern, yet retaining the external pincer type sprue cutter.

A brass mold was also made for the paper patched bullet and was intended to be used with the special swage. A shell sizer was made which had turned end plugs and was marked with the caliber of the die, the name "Sharps Rifle Co.", and the length of the cartridge case in inches. This shell sizer was made of round steel about three or four inches long.

Wood handled awl devices were made for removing the Berdan primers, and wood handled seaters were made for seating the wad at the proper depth in the case.

Wad cutters, which are hollow steel, were made in various calibers for cutting the wad to fit in the cartridge case over the powder. These were also made available by other companies. Some of these tools were undoubtedly made by sub-contractors.

A prize now eagerly sought by collectors is a leather cased set of sights for the Sharps rifles. Some of these cases are found in black morocco leather and some are in red. The case is stamped on the outside with the company name.

The sight cases had compartments for the windgauge front

sight, and for the inserts for the sight. There also was room for the vernier tang mid-range sight as well as the vernier long-stem heel sight. These sight combinations were made for the long range rifles and the Creedmoor type used in the long range rifle competition.

The sights were always removed from the fine target guns to prevent damage to the sights while transporting the guns. This practice led to the loss of the sights from the original guns. The sights were either discarded by subsequent owners or were sold separately from the guns themselves.

Occasionally, a powder can of the soldered tin type in brown or black japanned finish will be found bearing the Sharps Rifle Company label. Sharps did not make the black powder which these cans originally contained. The powder, while of a clean uniform grade, was purchased from the existing powder mills and packaged in the Sharps designed cans with the Sharps Rifle Company label. The same was true of the Sharps labeled percussion caps and, later, primers.

Telescopes used on Sharps rifles were usually Malcolm long tube telescopes of about 4 power with a very narrow field of view.

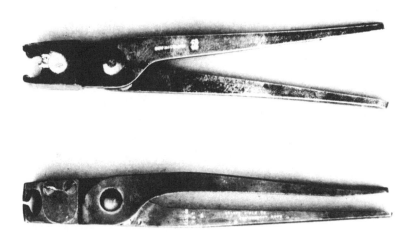

Sharps molds. Top, new model 1863 U.S. .52 and lower Bridgeport Conn. .45 Sharps. The top jaws were to be used to cut the sprue after the bullet was cast.

WHITNEY ARMS COMPANY

The Whitney Arms Company of New Haven, Connecticut, made and advertised the Burgess repeating rifle, the Whitney rolling block single shot rifle, and the Phoenix breech loading single shot rifle.

In 1878, their catalog carried a picture of the Whitney Creedmoor target rifle. The rifle was made in .38, .40, .44, .45, and .50 caliber central fire. The .44 could be chambered to take any one of the following loadings: 60, 77, 90, 100, or 105 grains of powder. The .40 was available in either the 50 or 70 grain loadings.

The Phoenix Schuetzen rifle was made in .38 or .40 caliber center fire. The stock was a German pattern polished, checkered stock and forend. The Schuetzen butt plate was nickeled. The barrels were available in 30 or 32 inch lengths and either half octagon or full octagon. The regular sights consisted of a vernier tang sight and a spirit level windgauge front sight.

The open rear V notch hunting sight was known as the "California sight".

The Target Rifles could have a Beach combination front sight, a spirit level windgauge front sight, and a vernier rear sight. The reloading tools for either rifle were listed extra at $5.00 per set. This set consisted of a cap extractor, a ball seater, and a bullet mold.

The Whitney Target Rifles were listed as a No. 1 Long Range Creedmoor in .44 caliber, a No. 2 Mid-Range Creedmoor in .40 caliber, and a Gallery Rifle in .22 rim fire long or short cartridge.

The Whitney reloading tools seemed to draw on several ideas, the re- and de-capper was of the hinged pliers type. The mold was a round cylinder solid type with a cupped pouring cut off plate. The cartridge loaders were of the straight line hand plunger type with a seating chamber and plunger. The seating chamber also acted as a resizing die.

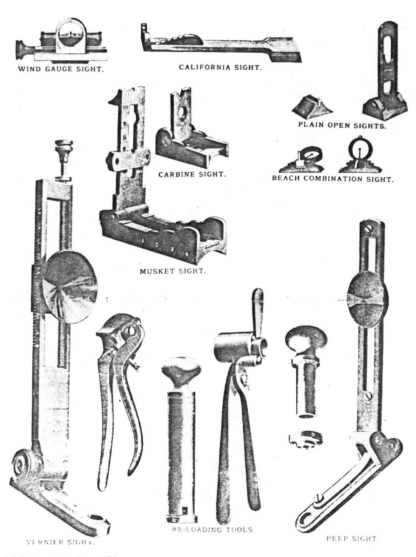

WIND GAUGE SIGHT.

CALIFORNIA SIGHT.

PLAIN OPEN SIGHTS.

CARBINE SIGHT.

BEACH COMBINATION SIGHT.

MUSKET SIGHT.

VERNIER SIGHT.

RE-LOADING TOOLS

PEEP SIGHT.

Whitney Arms Co., 1878

WINCHESTER REPEATING ARMS CO. SIGHTS

In regard to Winchester sights, the illustrations from the 1891 Winchester Repeating Arms Company catalog show the variety of sight combinations available to the purchaser of Winchester products.

The finest combination of sights on the Winchester rifles for the Schuetzen shooter was the front windgauge sight with a spirit level and the mid range vernier peep sight for the tang sight.

Today the sights most in demand among the single shot rifle shooters are the fine long range and mid-range vernier peep sights made by Winchester.

Both sights have the long flat hinged stem which is graduated with a fine screw elevation adjustment. Before trying to use the elevation screw. always slightly unscrew the eye cup to prevent stripping the thread on the screw. The sight has a base which is mounted on the tang of the rifle. the sight stem can be removed from the base if desired. This is why sights turn up with no bases.

Another very fine and rare sight has micrometer windage adjustments at the lower part of the elevation stem. This sight was developed and patented by J. W. Soule. The sight was very popular with the Walnut Hill, Massachusetts target shooters in the 1890's.

This sight was rather expensive to make and the only ones who bought it were the more affluent, serious shooters. Originally it was found on Winchester single shot rifles (when found at all).

As a result of the Lyman Number 103 and the Soule sight, as well as others which had windage in the base, the very fine Winchester windgauge front sights fell into disuse. Today these sights are avidly collected. If you use a windgauge front sight, remember the adjustment is, "move the front sight in the direction opposite from the direction you want the bullet to go!" This is just opposite from that taught marksmen today but today's admonition is for the adjustment on the rear sight, not the front.!

Today few target shooters would try to shoot with the plain open sights of yesterday. The peep sights advocated by Henry Lyman in the 1880's are still the best arrangement for iron sights.

The following pages are produced from the Winchester Repeating Arms Company, New Haven, Conn. catalog of March, 1891.

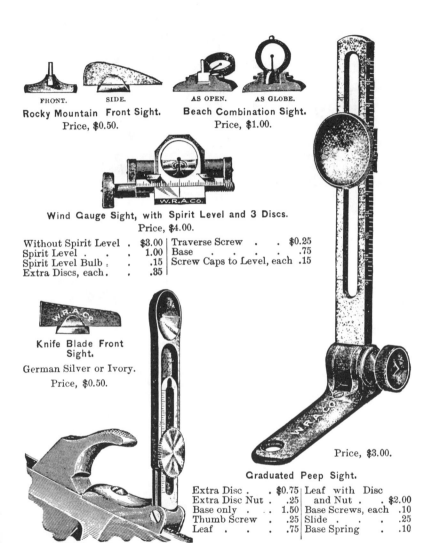

FRONT.   SIDE.
Rocky Mountain Front Sight.
Price, $0.50.

AS OPEN.   AS GLOBE.
Beach Combination Sight.
Price, $1.00.

Wind Gauge Sight, with Spirit Level and 3 Discs.
Price, $4.00.

Without Spirit Level .	$3.00	Traverse Screw . . $0.25
Spirit Level . . .	1.00	Base 75
Spirit Level Bulb : .	.15	Screw Caps to Level, each .15
Extra Discs, each . .	.35	

Knife Blade Front Sight.
German Silver or Ivory.
Price, $0.50.

Price, $3.00.

Graduated Peep Sight.

Extra Disc . .	$0.75	Leaf with Disc
Extra Disc Nut .	.25	and Nut . . $2.00
Base only . .	1.50	Base Screws, each .10
Thumb Screw .	.25	Slide 25
Leaf . . .	.75	Base Spring . .10

Price, $3.00. Adapted only to Mod. '73 Rifle.
Folding Peep Sight.

Winchester Express.
Front Sight. Price, $0.50.

Winchester Express.
Rear Sight. Price, $1.50.

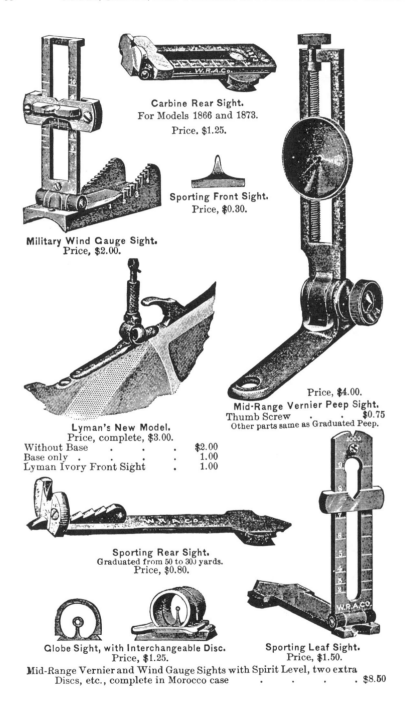

Carbine Rear Sight.
For Models 1866 and 1873.
Price, $1.25.

Sporting Front Sight.
Price, $0.30.

Military Wind Gauge Sight.
Price, $2.00.

Price, $4.00.
Mid-Range Vernier Peep Sight.
Thumb Screw   .   . $0.75
Other parts same as Graduated Peep.

Lyman's New Model.
Price, complete, $3.00.
Without Base   .   .   . $2.00
Base only   .   .   .   :   1.00
Lyman Ivory Front Sight   .   1.00

Sporting Rear Sight.
Graduated from 50 to 300 yards.
Price, $0.80.

Globe Sight, with Interchangeable Disc.
Price, $1.25.

Sporting Leaf Sight.
Price, $1.50.

Mid-Range Vernier and Wind Gauge Sights with Spirit Level, two extra
Discs, etc., complete in Morocco case $8.50

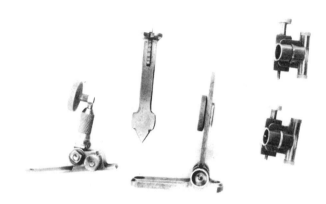

Winchester single shot sights #103 Lyman tang sight, Rocky Mountain rear open sight, Winchester tang sight (this is incorrectly called a vernier sight), without a vernier adjustment. Two windgauge front sights with vernier adjustment and leveling bubbles.

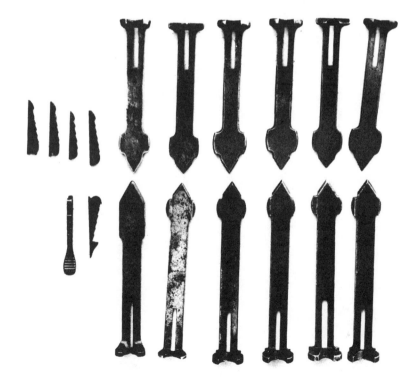

Open Ballard and Winchester rear sights which were called Rocky Mountain Sights.

CHAPTER 7

PRODUCERS OF CUSTOM MADE SIGHTS AND RELOADING TOOLS

BELDING & MULL

The original straight line lever action reloading tool was manufactured by the Belding & Mull Company of Philipsburgh, Pennsylvania, about 1926 or 1928. This tool was known as the #24 Straightline Reloading Tool. It de- and re-capped, neck resized, and expanded the case ready for reloading.

The powder charge was put into the case by using the Belding & Mull Visible Powder Measure. This was a very accurate powder measure designed to be clamped to the loading bench with a thumbscrew. The top was a round powder reservoir; the charge mechanism operated on a sliding principal; and the measured charge was dropped into the charge tube by operating the side lever.

Improved versions of the original #24 Straightline Reloading Tool were made, and model numbers 26 and 28 followed. Parts for these various models were not interchangeable.

The Belding & Mull bullet sizer was a bench mounted drive through die guide. Belding & Mull also offered a line of hunting and target rifle telescopes.

The company, like Ideal, put out a handbook type of catalog which gave reloading information and listed their tools.

Ideal full length hand resizing dies were sold with their tools for bench resizing of the cartridge case. Wilson resizing dies were also sold for this purpose.

BROWN'S VARIFORM RELOADER

D. Brown of 67 Clifford St., Providence, Rhode Island, advertised a compact lever hand held reloading tool in 1882-1883. In July, 1883 he advertised that .45 caliber was now available in the tool which could be loaded with paper patched or cannelured lead bullets.

November 10, 1883 the *American Field* announced that Brown had sold his patent rights to George W. Stafford & Co. of 68 Clifford St., Providence, Rhode Island.

Beginning with the advertisement of November 10, 1883 the advertisement for the Brown tool was in the name of the latter company. The advertisement also carried an endorsement letter from the pioneer gunmaker and dealer, Carlos Gove of Denver, Colorado, under date of August 28, 1883.

Advertisement as it appeared in the 1884 *Chicago Field*.

OTTO A. BREMER

Otto A. Bremer of San Francisco, California, made and marketed a round canister type powder measure which threw a double powder charge; one for priming the shell and the other for the main load.

The one illustrated is number 249. This number indicates that at least 200 to 300 were made and used.

Mr. Bremer made other reloading devices and also sights, but in a very limited number.

The powder measures were made and marketed during the late 1890's and early 1900's. The measures were made of brass and were nickel plated.

Bullet molds attributed to Bremer are of conventional design and are standard Ideal or Winchester pattern. Some of these may have been modified by Mr. Bremer with bullet cherries of his own design.

The plier type re- and de-capper shown in the photograph is clearly marked with Mr. Bremer's name.

Mr. Bremer also made very fine set triggers, stocks, and Schuetzen butt plates.

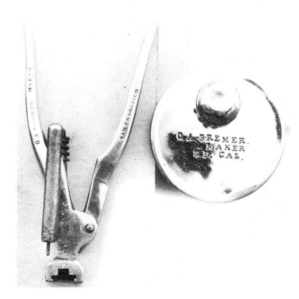

Re-and de-capper and a duplex powder measure made by O.A. Bremer of San Francisco, California. Capper — Collection of Michael Petrov, Alaska.

W. MILTON FARROW

W. Milton Farrow patented his rifle October 14, 1884, with an improvement issued October 25, 1887.

The accessories which he manufactured to go with these rifles were sights and Schuetzen type reloading instruments.

The Farrow micrometer peep and rear windgauge sight was a tang sight. I have only seen one of these sights and it was on an H. M. Pope .22 Stevens #44, Model 53 rifle.

The accompanying picture shows the sight on the Pope rifle.

The bullet seating tool was a straight line type with a turned wood knob.

The Farrow re- and de-capper was a hand held lever tool.

Farrow's molds were gang molds with an "automatic cut-off". The molds were cut to the shooter's specifications.

A swage was also furnished if wanted.

Farrow rear tang sight mounted on a 44 Stevens Pope .22 rim rifle. Collection Tom Lewis, Colo.

DEANE W. KING

Deane W. King of Denver, Colorado, in the early 1900's was known throughout the United States for his well constructed line of sights. Mr. King was a fine shot and competed nationally in the Schuetzen matches, establishing several never equaled national scores. He began his shooting career with the Colorado Rifle Club of Denver.

The King sights were manufactured by sub-contractors, Redfield Sight Company of Denver, also known as the Western Gun Sight Company, being one of the original manufacturers for King. Some of the early sights and duplex powder measures were also made by Schoyen and Peterson of Denver, Colorado.

Later, Mr. King had the sights manufactured in the San Francisco area where he moved his home and business.

In 1933, the Deane W. King Sight Company was located at 555A Howard Street, San Francisco, California. At that time, the company advertised in the American Rifleman, and the specialty was the King Red Bead Reflector front sight. The beads were 1/16 or 5/64 of an inch in diameter. The sight was also available with a triple bead for the more popular rifles of that period.

The King powder measure was a duplex Schuetzen style powder loading machine and was very well made. The measure is quite rugged and pleasing to the eye. To load with powder, the top is removed for access to the two charging reservoirs. The charge is set by a sliding opening which is retained by a set screw.

The King open rear rifle sights were advertised by the Pacific Gun Sight Company, San Francisco, California as well as by the Stoeger Arms Corporation of New York.

These sights were slot type adjustable leaf sights using the step adjusting device and adjustable discs. Special King open sights were made for the .30 U. S. Speingfields as well as the .30 U.S. Krag rifles.

Advertisements that I have for the King rifle sights date from 1913 to 1955 and are all basically the same open rear sights and bead front sights.

In 1913 a triple bead front sight was featured which had three beads mounted on a tiny axle. The bead head could be rotated to select the bead which would provide the best sight for the background.

ADOLPH O. NIEDNER

Mr. Niedner did not make very many special loading tools; those he did make were either for his own use or for experimental purposes. One of his ideas is shown here, a re- and de-capper which operates on a swinging fulcrum principal. He also made an adjustable charge powder measure which used insertable change cups to vary the powder charge.

Mr. Niedner did make some very fine straightline bullet seaters which were hand held. These seaters were made for smokeless powder cartridges and were designed for the precise alignment of the bullet and the cartridge case in order that the axis of the completed cartridge and that of the bore of the gun be as near perfect as possible.

Niedner also made reducing dies for the purpose of reducing a cartridge case to be used in one of his rifles which was especially chambered for one of his cartridge developments.

The dies were usually made and numbered in sets of three so that the cartridge case was reduced in size and in sequence to avoid distorted cases. These case sizing dies were hand held and were made to be used in a heavy bench vise.

On order, Mr. Niedner would also make cartridge case trimmers as well as bullet swages. Only one specimen of a bench Schuetzen de- and re-capper was ever made by Mr. Niedner. This tool was once in the author's collection. The principal was based on a rocking motion to de-prime then re-prime the case.

As for sights, Niedner made some very fine rifle sights in the 1920's. These sights were used on bolt action rifles; some were made for the mounting on bolt bodies which was popular at that time. Some of Mr. Niedner's sights are shown in detail in James V. Howe's book on gunsmithing.

Mr. Niedner also made a few steel tubed top mounted target rifle telescopes. These telescopes were high quality sights about 15 inches long with a ¾" tube and used Lyman telescope mounts and bases. The telescopes were made in 4 and 6 power.

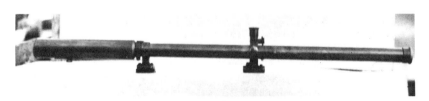

A. O. Niedner 3/4" rifle telescope 6X with a 1" objective. Modified Winchester-Mann-Niedner mounts. Bases are Mann-Niedner taper. Made at Malden, Mass.

These sights were made at Dowagiac, Michigan, as well as at his Malden, Massachusetts shop. Less than 6 of these telescopes are believed to have been made.

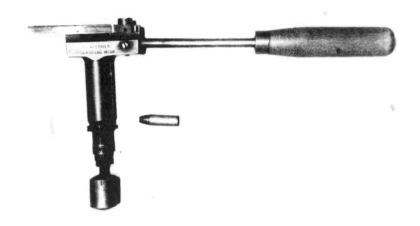

.38 Paper patch A. O. Niedner bullet mold.

A. O. Niedner Schuetzen bench type re-de capper for .32.40. Pushing back on handle as it was lowered caused the decapping pin to rise expelling the cap.

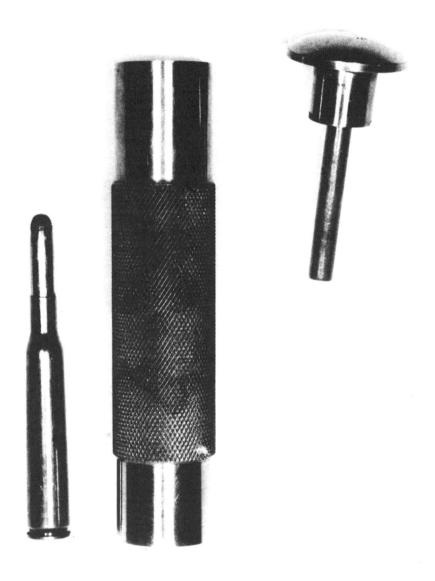

A. O. Niedner straightline hand-held cartridge bullet seater.

HARRY M. POPE

Mr. Pope used Ideal mold blanks which he cut for a particular caliber as ordered by his customers. The blanks were cut with Mr. Pope's own bullet cherries based on his design.

Pope also modified the cut off plate customarily found on Ideal molds to make a double cut off with the pouring spout on the point of the bullet instead of the base. From his own experiments, as well as those of Dr. Mann, he was convinced that any distortion or variation in the base would cause an unstable bullet; therefore, he eliminated distortion as much as possible by arranging the pouring from the point end of the bullet.

On Pope bullet molds, as well as those made on the Pope principle by the Stevens Arms Company, will be found a lubricating hole drilled in at the hinge pin with small letters "wax" if it is Pope and large letters "WAX" if it is Steven Pope. The bullet hinge was to be lubricated at the designated point with beeswax rather than oil.

Mr. Pope also made and marketed a duplex powder measure for Schuetzen shooters. This measure was made of tin, cylindrical in shape. When the measure was made by the Stevens Arms Company it was made of heavier material and nickel plated.

One of the handiest hand tools was that made by Pope for the de- and re-capping of the primer. The tool is easy to use, fail proof, and simplicity itself in design. The caliber is stamped on the rod, which is the decapping pin. These tools were also manufactured by the Stevens Arms Company as per their agreement with Pope when they bought him out and employed him in their factory.

Another one of the Pope accessories was a very finely made palm rest with a telescoping adjustment. This tool was also manufactured by Stevens and was copied by several others including a person in Ohio just before World War II who offered these as Pope Palm Rests. At that time, Mr. Pope was still active and, at his insistence, the tool and advertisements were withdrawn from the market. A number of these palm rests were, however, sold at that time.

H. M. Pope duplex powder measure with mounting spider. Coll. John Dutcher, Colo.

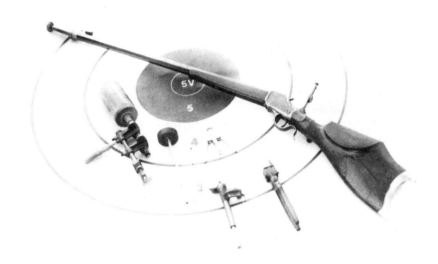

H. M. Pope, Hartford, Connecticut, High Wall Winchester Schuetzen rifle with tools. The butt plate is by Meunier and gun was made for competition in the Milwaukee, Wisconsin Club. Schoyen single cavity powder measure, bullet seater, Pope re-de capper, Pope double cut off mold and #187 Stevens-Pope bronze lubricating pump.

GEORGE C. SCHOYEN AND AXEL PETERSON

George C. Schoyen who was born in Norway, then emigrated to the United States, finally joined Carlos Gove, the Denver pioneer gunsmith in Denver, Colorado.

After working for Gove for some time, Schoyen worked on his own and in partnership with several others. Finally, he took in Axel Peterson whom he trained to follow in his footsteps.

Peterson was with Schoyen during the late 1800's and early 1900's when Schuetzen shooting and organizations were so popular. The Denver area shooters were particularly active during this period.

Schoyen developed tools and sights for the shooters, but it would be difficult to tell whether the work was Schoyen's or Peterson's. Therefore, the product that came from their shop' must be treated as a joint venture. After Schoyen's death, Peterson continued to make tools and accessories in the same pattern as that developed in the Schoyen-Peterson shop.

The nose pour molds which produce a bullet very similar to that of H. M. Pope are very distinctive. These bullet molds are usually found on Winchester handles although Ideal molds forms are also found.

The mold part of the tool was made by slotting the mold blocks and inserting a brass or bronze insert very much like putting a sight blank in a barrel slot. Then the blanks were cut on a lathe or small milling machine using a bullet "cherry". The bullet cherry is in reality a reamer with flutes milled on a formed steel bullet shape and is a cutting tool. The Schoyen-Peterson molds were point pour type. The base on these molds was always sealed with a half rounded steel plate attached to one side of the mold block with screws. This type of mold base closure was also previously used on the Sharps rifle molds.

Schoyen-Peterson molds made for Schuetzen rifle shooting used a bullet that was progressively larger from the nose to the base.

If bullets cast from a Schoyen-Peterson mold are intermingled with those cast from an H. M. Pope mold, it is almost impossible to tell which is which.

The bullet seating mechanism developed by Schoyen is quite distinctive. It consists of a handle with the cartridge case seater and a looped hook. This hook was placed over the take down pin head, and the case seater placed in the chamber. The wooden handled lever gave sufficient power to easily seat any bullet.

Some modern shooters insist that only bullets of bore size should be used in the old rifles. This is true if you are going to muzzle load the rifle and if you are going to use black powder!

Groove sized bullets are proper for loads using smokeless powders, and sometimes these seat rather firmly, so the Schoyen seater provided a means of breech seating these bullets with adequate leverage. This type of seater also minimizes bullet damage.

The Schoyen-Peterson re- and de-primer works on a double leverage principle. The original re- and de-cappers were made for the Denver Rifle Club members who were firing the .45 caliber guns at long range.

A few were made in .25 and .32 caliber for Schuetzen shooters.

One type of a duplex powder measure, and probably the first, was made utilizing two bottles which were removed from the measure after use and capped for carrying. The one bottle was for black powder, and the other was for a smokeless priming charge.

The smokeless powders used were such powders as Dupont #1 Rifle, Dupont Schuetzen, Dupont Bulk Shotgun, King's Semi—Smokeless, and others.

The second type of double cavity powder measure was a finely finished measure which had the formed metallic powder bowls permanently attached to the measure. These bowls were capped with screw on tops. This type of measure had a superior plate finish of nickel.

All Schoyen-Peterson tools are now very rare and are seldom found.

In regard to powder measures, there were apparently three types made.

A strange looking number of bronze casting and steel parts were obtained by a collector from the Peterson shop when it was finally disbanded; however, no one knew exactly what the parts were used for.

John Jamieson of Denver was given the job of trying to determine what the device was. After some trial and effort, John

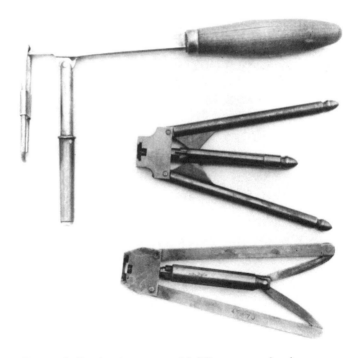

Schoyen-Peterson bullet chamber seater and 2 different types of re-de-capers.

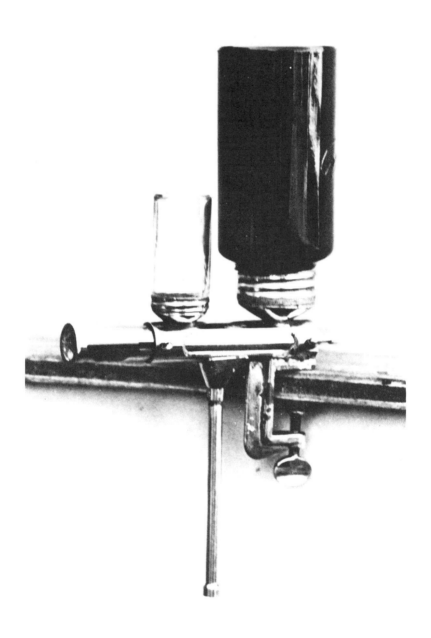

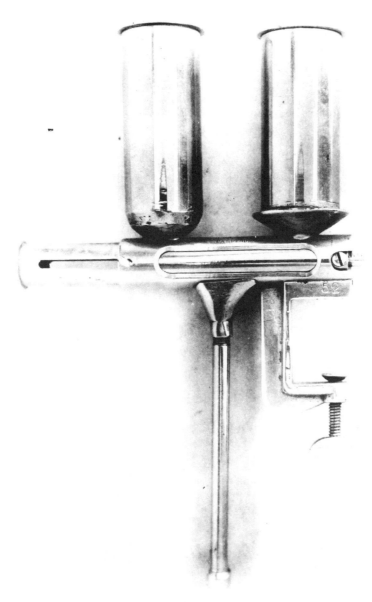

Schoyen-Peterson double cavity Schuetzen powder measure. There are two types, one with glass powder jars and the other is of all metal construction as is this one. Collection of John Dutcher, Colo.

was able to reassemble the parts, and a Schoyen-Peterson single cavity powder measure was recreated. A very limited number of the measures were made from the parts. How many were made by Schoyen-Peterson is unknown.

The first successful, graceful, and rare Schoyen double load Schuetzen measure was made in two types.

Mr. Peterson made many target .22 rim fire rifles as well as the standard Schuetzen center fire rifles. Some of these had a unique Peterson trigger mechanism added to the lower front of the block. This mechanism could be finely adjusted and worked more smoothly than a double set trigger. The mechanism was self setting.

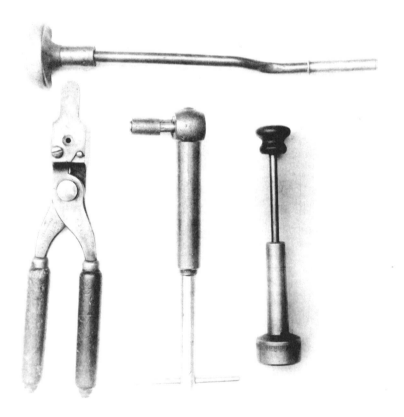

George C. Schoyen, Denver, Colo. tools to accompany one of his rifles. Top: breech bullet seater. Left: Winchester mold blocks with Schoyen bronze inserts. Middle: Schoyen grease pump for bullet lubrication. Right: Schoyen pattern bullet starter for muzzle loaded bullets.

SHEARD SIGHTS

W. F. Sheard of Tacoma, Washington, in the early 1900's, developed a front sight that proved popular with hunters. This sight was installed on many western hunting rifles of the 1910-1914 period.

The sight was a long blade type front sight with a gold and copper alloy bead installed on the end of the blade. This was sighted on by the shooter. The advertisements of the period claimed that the sight "will not blur and will show in the darkest timber and under the most unfavorable light".

In the 1930's the Sheard sight was listed in the catalog of the Marble Arms and Manufacturing Company of Gladstone, Michigan, as one of the sights manufactured by the company.

Marble sights were made as front sights, leaf rear sights and tang sights. The quality of Marble sights was and is excellent. The company is still in business today.

The American Rifleman listed in the August 1932 issue the four prominent makers of tang sights for single shot rifles as Lyman, Marble, Watson, and King.

F. WESSON TARGET RIFLES

Franklin Wesson manufactured breech loading firearms in Worcester, Massachusetts from 1859 to 1899. His rifles were well made but different from others, and most used cartridges which he himself developed and advertised.

The sights he used were varied and ranged from open blade front sights and Rocky Mountain notched rear sights to the long stem vernier rear sight of his Creedmoor rifles with spirit level windgauge front sights.

It is apparent, from an examination of some Wesson rifles, that he used Lyman sights as well as finely made target sights of his own make.

As for reloading tools, the only ones I have seen with Wesson rifles were similar to the Maynard rifle tools made by the Massachusetts Arms Company.

The re-and de-capper tong or plier type nickel plated tool shown in the photograph was with a cased Wesson rifle. There were no marks on the tool, but because of the circumstances it is presumed to be a part of the original tooling for the rifle.

Frank Wesson re-capper. No markings on tool but in a cased Wesson rifle set. Coll. Ronald A. Ogan, Ill.

J. D. WILKINSON

John D. Wilkinson was a maker of fine percussion rifles who was located at Plattsburg, New York. John worked with a brother and their products were sold to the public under the Wilkinson Brothers trade name.

In the early days they had their place of business at Keesville, New York. The business operated over a period of years beginning in or about the year 1857.

John was granted a patent for a single shot rifle with a rotating hinged breech block much like the English Snider action. The specimen I saw was .45 caliber with a 32 ¾″ octagonal barrel. The gun was a high grade sporting rifle. The front sight was a windgauge and the rear tang sight was a long stem vernier long range sight. The butt plate was crescent shaped. The lockplate bears the stamped name J. D. Wilkinson, Plattsburg, New York.

Duplex powder measure throwing a double charge of smokeless primer and black powder main load. Made by J. D. Wilkinson, Plattsburg, N.Y. Patented July 24, 1877. Collection of Michael Petrov, Alaska.

J. D. WILKINSON
MEASURING DEVICES FOR FILLING CARTRIDGES.
No. 193,434.   Patented July 24, 1877.

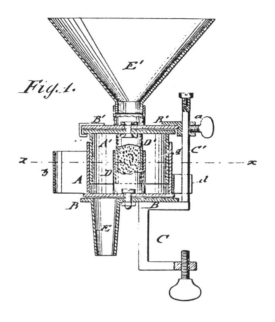

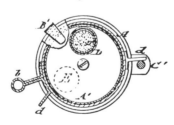

WITNESSES:

INVENTOR:
J. D. Wilkinson.
BY

ATTORNEYS.

The patent on this gun was issued August 29, 1871.

A very well made duplex powder measure which has been found with Marlin Ballard rifles has been identified as being made by J. D. Wilkinson of Plattsburg, N.Y. with a patent date of July 24, 1877.

This measure was mentioned in the 1887-1888 catalog of the Marlin Firearms Company, New Haven, Conn.

John D. Wilkinson was born in 1840 at St. Albany, Vermont. He served with the Union Army during the entire period of the Civil War.

Later he took an active part in the G. A. R. and in the Masonic Lodge.

From 1875 to 1919, J. D. Wilkinson was listed in the Plattsburg, New York, city directories as a gunsmith and locksmith at various addresses about the city. One of his locations was on Bridge Street where he carried on his trade of gunsmith. In the Plattsburg, N.Y., area he gained a reputation as a maker of fine rifles as well as being known for his marksmanship.

Mr. Wilkinson died November 12, 1918 at Plattsburg, New York.

AUGUST AND WILLIAM ZISCHANG

James Peek of Groton, New York, sent me his observations in regard to A. O. and William Zischang, father and son, who had a shop in Syracuse, New York, from 1879 to 1945.

August Zischang was considered to be one of the top four barrel makers in the United States. He had learned his trade in Germany, and his fine workmanship reflected his craftmanship.

In Mr. Peek's opinion, the older the Zischang mold, the longer and more awkward the handles are. Later molds have a thicker sprue cutter and more of a cavity at the sprue hole.

All the molds examined have been nose-pour with a possible exception of a hollow point mold. The bullet cherries from which the molds are cut seem to have been made with the dual purpose of cutting the mold cavity as well as the guide starter, loading rod, and perhaps a straight line type bullet seating die.

The adjustable Zischang mold is unique, for there is a plug in the base which moves to three different lengths by loosening a screw in the side of the mold and turning or raising and lowering until a tapped hole is felt, and then the screw is reset. The inside of the mold is marked 32-190-218-225 with index marks on the other side. Careful examination shows that the bottom of the plug is marked with a tiny "33" which is the clue to the mold. By reversing the plug it becomes apparent that it is tapered and slides neatly into the "218" mark.

The mold was made for a .32-40 rifle which was intended to be shot and then rebored to a .33. This was considered a good practice, for the rebored barrels were molecularly stabilized.

After the rebore the owner had only to reverse the plug to make a .33 two diameter bullet.

Tools and molds made by Zischang do not bear his name or any identifying marks.

The Zischang molds are made of bronze. The guide bullet starter which fits on the false muzzle has a "male" type locater on the end instead of the usual recessed opening.

Once you have the chance to carefully examine a Zischang mold, you will always recognize them because of the style and manufacture.

View of a short range bullet with a casting plug in the mold.

Mold by A. O. Zischange of Syracuse, New York. Courtesy of James Peek, Groton, New York.

I have a letter dated March 20, 1937 from the old time shooter, H. A. Donaldson, describing one of his favorite rifles, a .32-40 Zischang barreled Sharps-Borchardt.

The front sight is described as a special Zischang aperature windgauge front sight with six different inserts.

The rear sight is described as a vernier sight with micrometer elevation adjustment and a rocking motion giving windage to the sight. The disc had six holes of different sizes. Mr. Donaldson describes the sight as a Zischang sight and the finest he had ever seen.

Mr. Donaldson also had very high praise for the very good Zischang set triggers and the finely made Schuetzen butt plate.

In the letter he states that the Zischang mold is better than that of H. M. Pope and a square based bullet is more certain. Special note was made of the fine workmanship of the mold and the venting system.

MODERN VERNIER SIGHTS

One of the modern makers of very fine tang sights is Gaston Peccholt of Phoenix, Arizona. Mr. Peccholt worked in the arms factories at Liege, Belgium, where he learned his trade as gunmaker. Later he emigrated to the United States and finally settled in Arizona.

The vernier sights which he manufactured are very well machined. One sight is a duplicate of the Stevens Arms Company sight which was developed for the Stevens rifles by H. M. Pope. The sight has adjustments which includes stem screw adjustment for elevation and windage adjustments with two knurled knobs.

Vernier sights are adjusted by loosening the eye cup, making the adjustment, and then retightening the eye cup which has a screw-in piece which fits the sight bar.

Winchester vernier type tang sights were also made.

All of these sights are available through the Dixie Gun Works, Inc. at Union City, Tennessee.

Recently I examined a Soule model adjustable tang sight which showed excellent workmanship as good or better than original. This sight was made by an unknown maker in the Denver, Colorado area.

High quality workmanship does exist, but it is rare. Sights made today can be as fine as anything made in the past.

Another sight which is assembled or restored today is the vernier tang sight sold through the Navy Arms Company of New Jersey. The sight is made in Italy, and while it does not show the best of workmanship, it is a mass produced product which works and is reliable. There are two versions of this sight which could be called midrange and long range sights.

CHAPTER 8

FACTS AND HINTS ABOUT SCHUETZEN RIFLES

LOADING THE SHELL

In 1898, J. H. Barlow, the owner of the Ideal Manufacturing Company of New Haven, Connecticut, who had served in the Army during the Civil War, wrote the following in answer to shooters' requests for help in getting their rifles to shoot accurately with black powder:

"Some of our finest target shooters claim that to simply fill the shells with the common scoop and press the bullet down upon it, the results will be wild and irregular shoting. They have resorted to the loading tube. This is a brass tube with a funnel shaped mouth on one end and the other is fitted over the muzzle of the shell, and the powder is poured slowly through this tube, and in filling, each grain of powder seats itself more closely to its neighbor, thereby packing snugly and firmly which enables them to get more powder in the shell and still each kernel is kept in perfect form and not crushed, securing, as they claim, greater accuracy and regularity."

This loading tube was simply a brass tube or pipe of suitable small diameter and was from ten to twenty inches in length. Harry M. Pope used one on his own powder measure which was approximately eighteen inches long. Mr. Pope also used his when loading a duplex load. Today one must work up duplex loads using such powders as Dupont IMR powder #4227. Dupont #4759 can be used as well; both of these powders also make up very good loads when shot by themselves.

THE RIFLE BORE

Some shooters have almost a reverence for the old rifles; this is fine, but the guns were made to shoot, not just to look at, so try some safe loads of your own. I would stay away from some fast ignition powders which have been used in the past and which cause an enlargement of the bore just ahead of the cartridge case. A rifle must be fired many, many times before this condition will become apparent and, as in the past, the rifles loses its accuracy from such a condition. The only answer is to set the barrel back and rechamber it. The same is true of a barrel that is pitted. Once in a while one of these barrels will really shoot, but usually it requires that the barrel be rebored and rerifled for the next larger caliber. The old time shooters could have started with a .22 center fire, then had it recut to .25, to .28, then to .32, .33, .35, . 38, and finally a .39.

Remington and the Stevens companies, as well as many custom gunsmiths, offered reboring service, and it was an accepted method of restoring a rifle to service.

Primers today are such an improvement over those made in the past that one does not have to worry about the primer residue combining with the powder and ruining the barrel as it did in the not too distant past. Some barrels, however, have been damaged or ruined, and the only answer to the problem is a rebore. To a collector this is wrong, and a worthless barrel may mean more than one which is restored to shooting condition; again the question arises as to the purpose of the rifle; the answer of course is that it was made to shoot.

In my opinion, the finest pristine rifle is worthless if it will not shoot, just as is a piece which can be restored and is not.

When restoring a rifle, modern steels and methods can be used, but for the finish, try to use the old time methods. To me, an old rifle with a modern glossy blue and synthetic gloss finish on the stock is a horrible anachronism. Compared to today, the old methods were simple, and the methods assured success as well as beauty.

THE CHAMBER

The bore of the rifle is important, but so is the chamber; too often the chamber is overlooked. No two guns will have identically the same chamber even though cut by the same reamer. The variations are minor in most instances, but they are there, and this must be taken into account for your own rifle. Headspace, which is the tolerance allowable for a particular cartridge, is determined by the original fitting of the breech block and the chamber of the barrel. Substitution of a breech block, wear, neglect, changing a barrel can all affect the headspace tolerance and may be the difference between a safe rifle and one that is dangerous. Remember, when you have that rifle to your shoulder, and your face and eyes are within a few inches of the chamber, a mere tightening of the finger and you have an explosion exerting thousands of pounds of pressure per square inch on that chamber and breech. If the headspace, cartridge, powder load, bullet size are all correct, the bullet is propelled on its way and all is well; however, if one of these sensitive things is not right, the force of that explosion of thousands of pounds pressure can come back into your face. One moment of thoughtlessness can maim or kill, so don't take chances with vintage rifles that were safe when they were made. A lot of years have transpired between the manufacture of the older rifles and today's shooters.

CARTRIDGE CASES

Old brass cartridge cases are not safe to shoot. Yes, you may have fired some and nothing happened, but old brass becomes brittle and crystaline and the force of the chamber explosion can rupture that case and send the powder and particles back through the breech into your face.

The best thing to do is find a cartridge still made that can be made or formed into the case you need. Many modern cartridges can be so adapted. 30-30 Winchester cases can be formed into .32-40 and .38-55's, etc. For more information on making and using substitute cases, read the book *Cartridge Conversions* by George C. Nonte, Jr. published by the Stackpole Company of Harrisburg, Pennsylvania, 1961.

Some of the more unusual cases can be lathe turned of good brass and only a couple will be needed. Some old time "everlasting" cases were lathe turned. In some instances this term was applied to a solid head case instead of the early common folded head cases. All rifle cartridge cases are now made of solid head construction by the American companies. Do not use the old ' folded head cases; they are too weak and too subject to fracture.

A new or unused factory case fired in a rifle will expand to fit that particular chamber and, if you use the moderate velocity and pressure loads of a good target load, you can fire one case hundreds of times without resizing, providing you either breech seat the bullet into the bore ahead of the chamber or you seat the bullet in the case over a wad with just finger pressure. If you use a tool to seat the bullet in the cartridge case, the tool will crimp the case neck onto the bullet and these cases may require full length resizing.

Full length resizing of a brass cartridge case causes it to set up stresses within the brass thereby shortening the life of the case.

LEAD BULLETS

Lead bullets that are crimped into the cartridge case will not shoot accurately. There is no reason to use a crimped bullet in a single shot rifle. When the cartridge is fired the bullet must tear through the constricting force of the crimp, destroying its accurate size and shape. The accuracy of the bullet is gone before it ever strikes the lands and is on its way out the barrel.

Dr. Mann's experiments which resulted in the book, *The Bullet's Flight* in 1908, showed very markedly that any irregularity in the base of the lead bullet will cause it to be erratic in its flight. When casting your bullets, catch the bullet as it falls from the mold on a felt pad or folded cloth of some kind to protect the bullet from deformity.

After the bullet is lubricated, and there are several procedures for doing this, stand the bullets up in a small box and try to keep them in the order cast. Don't just heap your bullets together and then expect them to shoot well.

On the matters of molds, get a mold that is as perfect as you can get; buy a new one if possible. Old molds may be historic, but over the years they have been abused and neglected until most of them, as usually found, are worthless for shooting accuracy.

Lead must be properly united in the proportions you decide upon and in this matter there is great variation. Each shooter is emphatic on how this should be mixed; your own method will determine what is best for you. Most old time bullets are tempered by adding one pound of tin to twenty pounds of lead.

Make and cast one batch of lead from known composition; when the temper is right for you, keep a supply of these for test purposes. Use scrap lead and make some bullets of the same size as your control bullets. Put both these bullets in a vise and crush both of them at the same time; compare the bullets and then either add lead or hardener to your bullet metal until you get bullets of the same relative hardness as shown by your crushing test.

When casting bullets, use a piece of wood in convenient hand form to hit the cut off plate. Under no circumstances ever hit the cut off plate or the mold with a hammer or metal object. Don't pry a stuck bullet out of the mold for in doing so you may injure the sharp edge of the mold. The slightest dent on the inner surface edge of the mold will cause a bullet to "hang up" or stick.

Do not heat a mold in liquid lead for the slag will cause the mold to burn on its inner surface.

To avoid lead adhering to the strike off plate, on either side, touch it once in a while with a piece of beeswax.

Remember, molds must be *hot* to make good bullets.

To clean hot lead, put a piece of beeswax in the lead and ignite it. Stir the lead while this is burning. This is a dirty job and should be done in a well ventilated area. This is called fluxing the metal.

Often the question arises as to the size of the bullet. If your single shot rifle is "throated", that is, it is reamed to accept the exact shape of a certain bullet just ahead of the chamber, then that bullet should be used. To find out what the chamber and neck of the inside of the barrel looks like, make a sulphur cast of the chamber or use the special casting materials developed for this purpose. For further reference, consult a good book on gunsmithing.

But back to the bullet; drive a tight lead slug through the barrel and measure it with a micrometer. The bullet which you want to use is bore diameter, not groove diameter, plus one one-thousandths of an inch more.

Oversize bullets simply are swaged by the force of the explosion and changed from their original shape making an inaccurate bullet.

Almost all the bullets as cast are too large for the bore of the rifle they are being shot in. A breech seating tool is only made to seat a bullet bore size.

Old time bullets as cast have narrow driving bands and numerous grooves; modern bullets made for wide shallow grooves and narrow rifling, use fewer driving bands which have a greater bearing surface.

Paper patched bullets, the patching of which I have explained in more detail in *Schuetzen Rifles-History and Loadings*, requires a lead slug plus the thickness of the paper you are going to use. The diameter of the lead slug, plus the thickness of the paper should equal the diameter of the bore, or not over one-thousandths of an inch greater.

In the matter of rag paper, use a micrometer to choose it and try some various rag percentages for one seems to work better in a particular gun than another.

LUBRICATION OF BULLETS

There are as many recipes for bullet lubricants as there are shooters. One of the best methods of lubricating bullets is by dipping them individually into the hot lubricant and then setting them base down on a piece of metal to cool. Cover the grooves well with lubricant. Remove the excess with a close fitting cartridge case from which the head has been removed. This used to be called a "Kake Cutter".

Bullets forced through a sizing die will result in a deformed bullet.

The Ideal bullet lubricating machine No. 1 came out about 1898, and was extensively used for bullet lubricating. The best way to use this machine as well as the modern ones is to have a die one to three thousandths larger than the bullet and simply use the machine to lubricate the bullet without sizing or deforming it. In other words, cast your bullet to size with the mold and don't deform it with the sizer.

SHELL INDENTORS

Shell indentors were popular for a short time around the turn of the century, but they were not used by target shooters. As the powders changed, it was found that smaller amounts could be used in the cartridge case. Up until this time, the bullet was seated directly upon and was supported by the bulk of the powder. If smaller charges were used, a method had to be found to keep the bullet from falling back into the case. This was solved by the cartridge manufacturing companies rolling into the case a groove at the proper depth upon which the bullet could rest. The problems, however, arise once the cartridge is fired, for the force of the internal explosion will iron out this groove.

The shell indentor was a hand tool which had indented grooves in the shell holder and which permitted putting into the brass of the cartridge case a series of four little dot depressions at the exact depth which was desired to seat the bullet. A similar fluted decapping pin had to be used, of course, to slide by the indentation. Otherwise, the indentions would be ironed out.

My experience with the tool has indicated that it can be used for cartridges which cannot be neck resized. The closeness of a neck resizer does a more efficient job of holding the bullet. I have also found that after a few explosions of the cartridge, you have four very neat punched out neck holes.

SHOT CARTRIDGES FOR RIFLES

U. M. C. Rifle cartridge cases were furnished loaded with shot. Some cartridge collectors call these "wooden bullets". The shot cases were wooden sabots made to the same size as a regular bullet and were very thin. This wooden shot case was filled with a fine bird shot just as a shotgun cartridge. The sabots filled with shot were inserted into the rifle cartridge and crimped just as any other bullet and so today when one if found, it is a mysterious "wooden bullet".

POWDER MEASURES

Mechanical powder measures were used extensively from the 1870's on, so they were not something that is new to the shooting scene. One of the measures was an Ideal No. 6 which had a cast iron body. The measure had a double powder chamber and held one kind of powder which could be used as a primer and another kind of powder for the main load. This was known as a duplex loading measure. D. W. King, George C. Schoyen and Alex W. Peterson of Denver, Colorado all made duplex powder measures, as well as O. A. Bremer of California, Milwaukee Brass Company of Milwaukee, Wisconsin, and many others. All of them are interesting tools and still usable today.

The No. 6 Ideal powder measure was made late for the Schuetzen shooting. The Ideal measure which was used in the early 1900's was known as the No. 2 duplex Ideal powder measure patented in 1898.

RE—AND DE—CAPPERS

Once the cartridge case has been fired, the shooter then is faced with the problem of removing the fired primer. There have been many tools offered for sale over years to do this job, but perhaps the simplest is merely a short round rod which will fit to the bottom of the case with a small pin in it that will go through the primer hole in the bottom of the case. Insert the tool in the case with the small pin in the primer ignition hole and set the case on a piece of metal with a hole in the metal smaller than the case, this is used as an anvil, then tap out the primer with a small hammer. This method is fast and simple and can be used at the bench while you are shooting or when decapping a large number of cases. A well made properly hardened decapping pin will remove U.S. government crimped in primers easier and more quickly than any other method I know of.

Custom gunsmiths over the years have made various re-and de-cappers including H.M. Pope, A.W. Peterson, George C. Schoyen and many others. The Ideal Company made two re-and de-cappers; one a hinged device which was known as the Ideal No. 1 and a straight line re-and de-capper for bench mounting known as the Ideal No. 2 model.

I never liked the No. 2 model, for it was not as convenient to use as the hinged or pliers type capper.

BULLET SEATERS
The best accuracy with lead bullets is obtained by seating the bullet into the barrel ahead of the case and then inserting the loaded case separately.

The Ideal Company made two models known as the Ideal Bullet Seater No. 1, and No. 2.

The No. 1 seater was a heavily constructed seater which gave enough tool to seat the tapered bullets as well as ones made of harder alloys. The No. 1 seater was designed by Dr. Walter G. Hudson, a famous shooter in the early 1900's.

The No. 2 seater was a much more lightly constructed seater and it had a long graceful handle which had the seater on a separate section of the handle. This section slid the bullet in a straight line into the chamber rather than depending upon the directly exerted force. This tool was made for any cartridge the shooter wished to order from .22 on up.

The bullet seating tool was made to seat the bullet one thirty second of an inch ahead of the cartridge case. The No. 2 seater, however, could be adjusted by a knurled nut to seat the bullet to the depth desired by the shooter.

THE PALM REST
The palm rest is not a toy or just another gadget. If properly adjusted it equalizes physical differences and enables the rifle to be held and aimed with the most comfort and reliability. Muscular tension or reaching out for a palm rest too far from the action will cause a shooter's unsteadiness and affect the score.

Get into position from which you will shoot your offhand score and direct your rifle toward the target. As you settle into a comfortable position close your eyes. When you open them the rifle should be pointing at a level with the target.

If the palm rest is too close to the receiver the holding hand has to support too much weight. This is true because the center of gravity is not centered on the palm rest support.

If the palm rest is too far forward the weight of the rifle forces the palm rest open and away from the body. The ideal rest weight should lock the palm rest in position without pulling the shooter's arm toward the body.

The palm rest should rest on the heel of the hand with the fingers lightly closed on the grip of the rest.

The grip of a palm rest can vary in shape from a round flattened grip to a finger fitting custom grip made for the individual shooters. The important thing is the grip should be made to make the shooter more comfortable and give more reliability in the shooting stance.

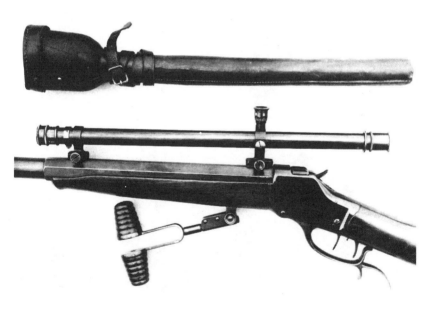

Winchester leather telescope carrying case. A5 Winchester rifle telescope and mounts. Winchester Special Order early Schuetzen straight grip, double set trigger, high wall Winchester .32-40 single shot rifle. Early pattern grip type Winchester palm rest with Winchester lever and forend base. Later palm rests were with a straight stem and threaded screw adjustment with base like the H. M. Pope type.

H. Pope and A. O. Niedner made palm rests with a sliding nut adjustment on the stem which provided positive adjustment. George Schoyen and A. W. Peterson used a threaded locking adjustment. Winchester grips were distinctive and easily identified. (see photo) Individual makers and shooters made their own formed grips and, although there is a similarity in form, the appearances vary.

Joseph Singer of California made palm rest fittings which were very distinctive.

Palm rests had not become the vogue when Ballards were made, therefore there were no company-made rests. Any Ballard having a palm rest is the result of the work of a custom gunsmith.

Winchester made two company palm rests, one with a threaded and sliding stem and the other a double grip type. The forend fittings were Winchester made.

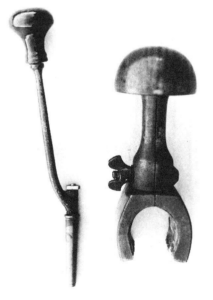

Wooden palm rest made to slide over forearm and clamp in position, obviously made by a Swiss or German craftsman. To the left is an adjustable Ideal breech seating tool to seat the bullet in the chamber ahead of the cartridge case for Schuetzen type shooting.

Two types of palm rest stems by H. M. Pope. One on left has a sliding nut adjustment and the one on the right has a threaded screw adjustment. Collection John Dutcher, Colo.

Stevens made the Pope type palm rest which was fitted to their Schuetzen rifles as company furnished equipment. The rest and fittings could also be purchased and fitted to the individual's rifle.

SET TRIGGERS
There are double set triggers, single set triggers and standard single trigger mechanisms.

The double set triggers are not new. The use of double set triggers was found on early Pennsylvanian flint lock rifles. This trigger mechanism consists of two triggers. Through a bar arrangement the rear trigger is pulled back under tension until the front trigger mechanism snaps into place. The trigger is now set or cocked and a slight touch on the front trigger discharges the trigger which strikes the rear and causes the firearm to discharge. The advantage in a double set trigger is that the gun responds to your wish at the moment the sights are properly aligned. The front trigger can usually be adjusted for lightness by a very small screw in the lock plate near the front trigger.

With single set triggers the trigger is pushed forward to cock it. Single set triggers were made by most of the single shot rifle makers. Some were developed and made by individual gunsmiths for rifle actions which were worked over for the target shooters. Some set triggers like the Sharps for the 1878 hammerless were not exactly successful.

CHEEKPIECES
Checkpieces on long guns originated in Europe centuries ago. The cheekpieces appears on wheellock guns as well as on ancient crossbows. Since the Pennsylvanian flintlock was made by the German and Swiss gunmakers who had come to this country the cheekpieces carried over to the flintlock guns, then the percussion sport guns and eventually to the cartridge guns.

The cheekpiece probably reached its zenith during the days when Schuetzen rifles were at their finest.

The so-called Tyrolean cheekpiece was large and deeply curved and was fitted to the face of the shooter. Some have compared it to a cradle. This may be beautiful, but it is worthless on a rifle. As the rifle is fired the curved cheekpiece acts as a plow with the recoil turning the muzzle in the direction opposite the curve.

The Swiss cheekpiece is similar to the Bavarian but is longer.

The Bavarian and the Swiss cheekpieces were commonly used on the "Kentucky" rifles and permitted a straight line recoil.

The German cheekpiece is a rounded oval and is rather short. It, too, has no "dish" to its set but permits a straight recoil.

The cheekpiece on a modern rifle is an adaptation of the German and Swiss form. The modern cheekpiece is oval in shape, but blends smoothly into the stock at the front and extends well to the rear of the stock. The cheekpiece aids in resting the comb of the stock against the cheek at the right height and permits the rifle to recoil in a straight line.

Engraved #44 Stevens-Pope .22 rim fire rifle with M. Farrow rear tang sight, double set triggers and inset walnut blocks on trigger guard. Collection Tom Lewis, Colo.

High Wall 1885 Winchester Single Shot rifle by H. M. Pope. Note the palm rest, the guard lever, and the shape of the cheek piece on the pistol grip stock. The tang sight is a Pope sight. Double set triggers. Collection John Dutcher, Colo.

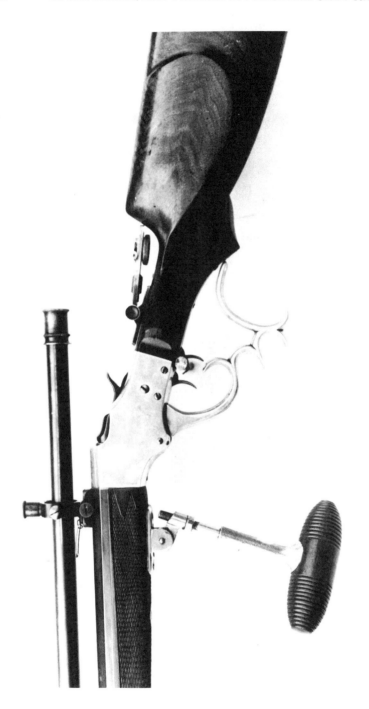

#44 1/2 Stevens Pope rifle, A5 Winchester target mounts. Double set triggers, Pope finger lever. Joseph Singer palm rest and grip. Tang sight is Stevens. Note the shape of the cheek piece on the pistol grip stock.

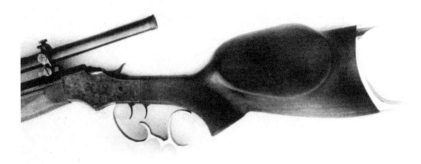

Buttstock of a John Jamieson 44 1/2 Stevens .22 rim fire rifle. Telescope is Jamieson, mounts are Stevens. Jamieson butt plate, stock, trigger lever and double set triggers. Note the German type cheek piece.

CHAPTER 9

LEAD BULLETS AND LUBRICATING WADS*

by N. H. Roberts

A cast iron pot is needed in which to melt the lead; heat this over a gas or gasoline stove and keep the metal at as uniform temperature as possible while casting the bullets. After the lead and tin is melted, drop in a piece of rosin the size of a large pea and stir until it is burned off; which fluxes the metal, makes it flow better and fill the mould evenly each time. The Ideal Bullet Dipper is the best to use in pouring the melted lead into the mould and insures filling properly, thus producing perfect bullets. Strike the cut-off with a piece of wood so as to cut off the sprew, which is dropped back into the melting pot; turn the mould to one side and tap it with the piece of wood to jar the bullets out of it. Drop the bullets on a thick pad of cloth to cool - not onto a board as that would dent them and prevent their shooting accurately. After casting a supply of round balls and bullets, inspect them carefully and reject all that are wrinkled or imperfect, as it is only wasting good powder to shoot imperfect bullets.

The bullet mould has a cut-off and will cast nice bullets when properly managed. It is impossible to use these old moulds as they are issued, since they have iron handles that burn the hands when they are heated as is necessary to cast good bullets. Wood handles must be fitted to them or one can go to the garage

---

* Letter from N.H. Roberts, sone of this also appeared in the March 1944, *Hunting and Fishing.*

and get two pieces of radiator hose having a ½ inch hole and each about five inches long. Then slip a piece of this hose over each handle of the mould and you can cast bullets comfortably without burning your hands. When the rubber handles get hot, dip them in cold water when you have a bullet in each cavity of the mould to prevent getting any water in these.

Before starting to cast bullets all grease and oil must be thoroughly wiped off of the outside and inside of the mould; be sure to get this all out of the cavities, else the bullets will all be imperfect and useless. Wet a piece of cloth in cigarette lighter fluid, or carbon tetrachloride, and wipe out each bullet cavity with this in order to fully remove all grease and oil. Then heat the mould hot enough to sizzle like a hot flat iron when touched with a wet finger; then cast a supply of bullets. If the mould casts imperfect bullets, smoking inside with the flame of a match or candle, generally prevents this and the bullets will then come out perfect. The bullets should be cast from pure lead, not hardened to any extent, although some rifles give the best accuracy with bullets cast from a mixture of three pounds of soft lead and one ounce of tin, or one ounce of old type metal. Try different mixtures to get the best results in your rifle.

The lubricating felt wads mentioned are made from an old hat; cut the hat into strips about three inches wide by six inches long and soak them in a hot mixture of equal parts of beeswax and vaseline, or beeswax and sperm oil, for cold weather use. For summer use, make the lubricant about 2/3 beeswax and 1/3 sperm oil or vaseline. After the strips of felt are thoroughly filled with the lubricant, remove them and hang up to dry for an hour or more; then cut the wads with the proper size wad cutter. Cardboard about 1/16 inch thick may be used in place of the hat felt and treated in this same way for making the lubricating wads, which are necessary to prevent leading the bore of the rifle. Another method to prevent this leading is to place a card wad over the powder in each casing; then place a strip of IPCO Colodial Wad sheet over the case and press with the finger thus cutting a wad of this in the case before seating the bullet. The IPCO Colodial wads come in different thicknesses, but I use those .033 inch thick and have no leading of the bore even after shooting fifty shots or more.

CHAPTER 10

CAST BULLET LOADING
BY H. GUY LOVERIN*

H. Guy Loverin was a shooter-experimenter in the 1930's and 1940's whose bullet designs were adopted by the bullet mold manufacturers.

One of his designs was the Ideal No. 225438 gas check 44 grain Hornet bullet. Another was the 154 grain .30 caliber gas check mold made by Modern Bond No. 311910.

Mr. Loverin made bullet molds of his own design and was located at Lancaster, Massachusetts.

The American Rifleman Dope Bag in August, 1942 commented, "We have never obtained a poor or unseccessful bullet from Loverin's molds and sizing machines."

The following information is from a letter Mr. Loverin wrote in 1964.

"The best diameter for cast bullets used in rifles is a difficult topic. The hardness or temper of the bullet metal and the shape of the bullet have a great bearing on choice of diameter.

Bullets actually lengthen in firing, as I have found by measuring many bullets fired for recovery in cotton. Therefore, to deliver a bullet in as perfect shape as possible it should have bearing bands its entire length except for a short, rather blunt nose. Such bearing bands on a long bullet should measure about .301 inches at the front (for a caliber .30 rifle) with the following

---

* Copy of letter from Guy Loverin which also appeared in March 1964, American Rifleman.

bands increasing in diameter. Body of the bullet should be cast of the usual diameter and sized to .311 inches.

Bullets made to this design, and cast of an alloy of 1 to 20 tin and lead, have always performed well for me. The rifling bands cut easily into the forward bands of a bullet made of this soft alloy when the cartridge is loaded into the rifle.

While bullets of this design can be obtained only by modifying some existing mold, they are approximated by the Lyman bullets No. 311466 and 311467, weighing 155 grs. and 180 grs. respectively. These bullets have bands nearly their full length, with the forward bands of reduced diameter for alignment in the rifling.

But, such a bullet of hard metal will simply be pushed back into the cartridge case when loaded into the rifle, unless cast in an undersized mold. If hard bullets are used I suggest .308 inch molds, or .309 inch at most. Also, if a long-pointed spitzer-type bullet is preferred, at .311 inch diameter it would have to lengthen so much that it might throw the long point out of balance. This type will do best cast .308 inch to .309 inch and lubricated without sizing.

In either style the grease grooves should be extremely shallow. Caliber .30 molds can be drilled out to .297 inch, or .281 inch it if is desired to keep the gas-check shank. The remaining shallow grooves carry enough lubricant and leave the bullet stronger. I compared the shooting of bullets cast in a mold so drilled (which increased the bullet weight 4½ grs.) with bullets made before drilling. Bullets from the altered mold made groups about half the size of those from the mold in its original form.

For bullets with bands nearly the full length as described, I have found that best results would be obtained with an alloy of 1 to 20, using only lead and tin. In this comparatively soft alloy, such bullets should have one or more oversized bands to give suitable resistance. The best place for these large bands is the middle of the bullet. This can be accomplished in 2 ways - by buying undersized molds and enlarging the middle band; or by using conventional molds and carefully sizing the foreward end of the bullet to .308 inch and rear end to .310 inch. The latter is the system I am now using with best results.

If in casting the bullets are not completely filled out, weigh the bullets and use only the heaviest ones. It is better, however, to make them all perfect. Keep the metal and the mold up to correct operating temperature. Leave the dipper connected to the mold for sufficient time, and an equal length of time for all bullets. Long bullets especially require that the cooling, shrinking bullet be fed metal from the dipper until it has solidified.

In most cases rifles shoot best groups when fired with the powder forward in the powder space, against the base of the bullet, though the bullets may strike lower on the target. When the powder is back at the primer the base of bullets recovered from cotton has a rough appearance as though the grains of powder had been blown against it. When the powder is forward at the base of the bullet, the base of the recovered bullet is clean.

Plain-base bullets also shoot well.

There is no need of a filler with light loads. Simply lower the muzzle before each shot to give a large air space in front of the primer.

Cast bullets are ordinarily used within 100 yards. However, using the above gas-check bullets and light loads I have fired scores of 48x50 on the standard military targets at both 300 and 500 yards.''

CHAPTER 11

GUNPOWDERS AND PRIMERS

In the United States, in the latter part of the 1800's, the standard gunpowder was of the kind known as "black". The powder made by the Dupont Powder Company of the United States was the standard of the world.

Many shooters, however, insisted that the Curtis and Harvey gunpowder of England was the best.

Later, smokeless gunpowder came into use and the experimentation associated with a new development began. Because of the method of reloading which had been developed over the years by some shooters results with smokeless powders were sometimes disastrous.

I recall many years ago when buying a fine old percussion muzzle loading rifle from an old farmer, how he cautioned me not to use much of the powder in the gun because it sometimes blew the nipple out. The powder he gave me was black all right, but it was a smokeless powder known as "Sharpshooter" and the load he used was a healthy load for a cartridge gun, let alone an old soft iron barreled muzzle loader.

As the powder companies labored to tame the smokeless powders, they also had to find a new type of primer to detonate the powder. Regardless of how well the cleaning was done of rifle barrels, the primer residue combined with the smokeless powder to form an acid which immediately attacked the steel of the rifle bore. This is the reason why so many rifles used in the early 1900's have pitted barrels.

Remington Arms Company of Ilion, New York, was the first to develop a non-corrosive primer. Their cartridges were marketed under the "Kleanbore" trade name. Finally, all U. S.

ammunition companies changed over to a noncorrosive primer. The U. S. armed forces arsenals, however, continued to use a non-mercuric corrosive primer through World War II when even they changed over to a non-corrosive primer.

Today, any company still in the powder or ammunition business is only interested in making money based on a huge market. This was not always true and despite the fact that the Dupont Company was big, it still was responsive to the needs of the shooters of the United States who had, in turn, contributed to its corporate wealth.

Because of the government anti-trust laws, Dupont had to establish independent powder producing companies such as the Hercules and Atlas Powder Companies in 1911. Because of the needs of the United States for powder produced by Dupont for national defense, the smokeless powder plants were to be retained by Dupont intact.

Dupont and Hercules both developed reliable gunpowders which were accurate, and have served the shooters needs.

Some of the early Schuetzen powders developed by Dupont were Rifle No. 1, Schuetzen Smokeless, and Dupont Bulk Smokeless Powder. These powders have given very reliable results when properly used in Schuetzen loadings.

Today, Dupont IMR4227 and IMR4759 are used with good results.

Another powder company which produced a powder used in combination with Dupont powder was that of the King Powder Works located on the little Miami River, 23 miles northeast of Cincinnati, Ohio.

The King Powder Works was formed and run by a J. W. King who produced a high velocity, low pressure, semi-smokeless powder which replaced black powder. This powder was first patented January 17, 1899, and was made in the various granulations as was true of black powder.

Charles W. Rowland, the old time shooter of Boulder, Colorado, who made such fantastic groups, was a firm believer and user of King's semi-smokeless powder as a primer because of its reliability and uniformity of ignition.

Today, some Schuetzen users use Dupont IMR4227 or 4759 as priming charges for black powder which is used as the main charge.

Personally, I get the best results in my Pope and Schoyen rifles by using the loadings recommended by Mr. Rowland in his letters to Mr. Pope as shown in my book *Respectfully Yours, H. M. Pope.*

As for primers, the advancement made in stability, reliability, and dependability by the private cartridge manufacturers has been truly remarkable. Many of the old Schuetzen rifles have peppered barrels because of the corrosive action of the primers on the steel in the bore of the rifle. All black powder cartridges of the old single shot rifle days are loaded with mercuric corrosive primers.

If you buy a few old cartridges and intend shooting them in one of your rifles, always unload the cartridge, take out the powder and the primer, and dispose of them safely. Reload using new powder and a modern non-corrosive primer.

If you fire one of the old time cartridges as is, the mercury from the primer will amalgamate with the brass cartridge case and make the brass brittle. The corrosion from the primer will immediately attack the steel in the bore, so don't be tempted.

Remington arms pioneered the improvement in primers with their "Kleanbore" formula. Winchester followed with "Staynless" and other companies followed suit.

The U. S. Army continued with corrosive, but not mercuric, primers up until World War II. By the time the war was over, non-corrosive primers were in use in military firearms.

Up until 1942, the .45 ACP cartridge manufactured by the Federal Arsenals used a primer different in size from the commercially produced .45's.

The old time Union Metallic Cartridge Company used a "U" stamp on their 1 ½ small rifle primers as well as on the 2 ½ large rifle primers; this was discontinued later. Winchester had a "W" on their #1 ½ primers which were made under a patent date of October 1, 1878. Large caliber rifle cartridges, after the Berdan primers were discontinued, were primed with a #5 ½ two part primer made like a shotgun shell primer. The patent dates on this primer were October 1, 1878 and September 9, 1884. This primer did not continue in use for a very long period of time; the regular cup and anvil coming into use superceded this primer. Many early primers were formed of copper rather than the brass alloy of present use.

Today, due to the control exercised, all primers made by the leading cartridge companies can be used with expectation of accuracy. It becomes simply a matter of individual preference. Primers from Europe do not have a long storage period reliability and they all develop misfires in a much shorter time than do U.S. made primers. This, of course, affects the accuracy of the cartridge since the ignition is not constant.

When I make the statement in regard to the accuracy factor of all U. S. primers, I do not mean to imply that all primers will perform in the same manner with your loading and particular gun. The primer directly effects the ignition and burning rate of the powder which in turn effects the ballistics of a particular load. Primer variation will cause a variation in pressure.

As one who fired hundreds of moderate and reduced loads, I have determined that the time pressure rate of the reduced powder load is just as critical as with a full load although the pressure factor may not be as great.

One of the most stable primers for shooting the single shot center fire cartridge rifles was the older Remington 2½ nickeled primers marked "For Black and Smokeless Powder Cartridges".

Changing from one brand of primer to another will cause a variation in the accuracy of a particular loading.

The variation in the pressure used to seat a primer will also cause a variation in accuracy by causing a variation in the timing of ignition.

The vent hole size variation will also cause a variation in ignition timing. This is one reason why the use of one case only is recommended for consistent shooting. The flash hole or primer vent hole is the same from shot to shot. The case is fire formed to fit the chamber, giving a uniform gas seal. By seating the bullet into the breach with one particular seating tool, a uniform shooting depth is insured.

If fixed ammunition is used, you have a number of variables which are eliminated by the use of the one case.

Some shooters recommend fillers which are to be put into the case over the powder to hold the powder in place. Any fillers which are used are themselves the cause of an uncontrolled variant because of their effect on the burning rate of the powder. The fillers affect the density of the powder load. The rate of the burning of the powder is increased, but the absorption by the filler of the heat produced will also cause an effect as well as the weight of the filler which must be added to the weight of the bullet while it is moving through the barrel. Remember that as air space is decreased, pressure is increased when using smokeless powders.

Lead bullets which are used in fixed ammunition and are

crimped into the cartridge case so that they may be used in magazine type rifles, have no place in single shot rifle shooting if accuracy is expected. Crimped bullets cannot be crimped into the case uniformly under ordinary reloading conditions, the result, of course, is inaccuracy due to a retardation of certain parts of the bullet in its forward movement at the time of powder explosion in the case.

In regard to the bullet itself, there seems to be a constant argument between those who feel that the bullet should ride free on the lands, (be bore size) and those who feel that it should be .001 of an inch larger than the groove diameter.

Fast acting, smokeless powders and black powder will give a sledge hammer effect to the base of the bullet and will seal the bore by deforming the base. A bullet of groove diameter will already be seated in the rifling and the progressive powder explosion will cause an increasing velocity as it is forced down the bore. As to which size bullet is best for your rifle, only experimentation will tell which shoots best for you. In any event, if you are only interested in increased velocity, shoot a modern rifle and forget the detailed experimentation that is necessary with moderate loads and lead lubricated bullets.

One other factor which should be mentioned here is, to provide yourself with some shade when you are doing experimentation or shooting the single shot rifle. Do not allow your powder measure to set in the sun. The same is true of fixed ammunition. Don't allow it to lay on the shooting table in the sun. The heat will cause unsafe variations as the powder breaks down and the pressure and rate of burning becomes erratic and unsafe.

Some shooters use a light card wad over the powder. Since the light Schuetzen loads will not fill the case, a plunger type knobbed wad seater should be used so that the wad which you have cut with a wad cuter will be seated at a uniform place in the case. A wad over the powder will also give a more uniform ignition. The alternative to not using a wad is to elevate the rifle so that the powder is forced to the rear of the case and the rifle gently lowered to the line of fire. This must be done uniformly from shot to shot.

Some writers have stated that the blotting paper wad, which was cut with a standard steel round wad cutter, was pressed into the mouth of the case with the thumb and then a 1/16" to 3/32" wax wad was thumbed over the paper. This is true if you use black powder which fills the case! However, if you use a light smokeless charge and use the above instructions you will still have a loose unconfined powder charge and the rifle must be elevated before firing to seat the powder back in the case so that the powder ignition will be somewhat uniform. It is best, in such situations, to place the postal card type wad lightly and directly on to the powder charge. Wads can be cut with leather tool circular cutters which are made much as the old time cutters were made.

The argument is used that card wads act as a gas check and give increased velocity. The increased velocity is minimal but the true purpose is to give uniform powder ignition.

In regard to duplex loads, I am a firm believer in using the duplex or Schuetzen loading when using black powder. The shooting is cleaner and the accuracy is improved. I do not recommend mixing powders when using smokeless powder loads. If you are going to use Dupont 4759 or 4227 powders for example, find a recommended loading for the caliber of your rifle, drop it 5 grains and work up a load by gradually increasing the load in your gun until you get some accuracy and then vary this load until you find one that is satisfactory. You will also find that your particular gun will shot its best with only one type of powder and primer and that is what lends interest to the single shot rifle shooting.

Ordinarily, powder can be measured for the old type calibers. It is not necessary to weigh each charge as do the high velocity bench shooters. Because I grew old with the Ideal tools, I have always preferred the Ideal powder measures. Today, the #55 measure serves as well as the old #6. In any case, become familiar with your measure and how it works. Be sure to check the charge thrown with a powder scale to insure a correct and safe setting.

CHAPTER 12

OFFHAND RIFLE SHOOTING*

by Harry M. Pope

This is written with the hope that it will help riflemen generally to make better offhand scores; it is based upon many years of shooting and as many years' association with the best offhand shooters that this country has ever produced, as well as my long experience in rifle-making, and may help others to ultimate victory.

THE OFFHAND POSITION

This will vary somewhat with individuals, but it must be perfectly natural, easy and free from muscular strain. The weight should be evenly distributed on both legs; they should be straight and not too far apart. Legs spread too far means muscular strain, while in a proper position the bones should carry the weight. As the writer stands, the feet are at an angle of about 60°, the left foot about 50° with the line of fire, the right a little back or square to the line of fire, the heels 7" apart. Don't straddle.

In getting into shooting position, it is extremely important that one gets so set that a natural, easy position directs the rifle at the bullseye. Therefore, in aiming let the rifle come to its natural position. Then, if looking over the sights it is right or left, rock backward, letting the left leg hang, swing the body so the rifle will

---

* Written by H.M. Pope for the February 1, 1906 issue of *Shooting and Fishing*.

point at the bull, then rock forward, letting the right leg hang down naturally, and you will now find that the rifle points itself at the bull merely by assuming a perfectly easy position without muscular strain. If not properly set, of course, one can direct the rifle to a considerable angle at either side, but when the nerves relax control of the strained muscles to the slightest degree, the muscles assume a natural position and the rifle swings off. A little practice lets one get set at the proper angle, so very little of this setting is necessary.

AIMING AND PULLING

In a match of considerable length one should never try to pull every shot dead center. It can't be done, and to try to do so only results in fatigue and wild shooting. No matter how expert, one practically never holds perfectly still; there is always a swing or tremor. Don't outhold your wind. Try to pull the first time the sights swing slowly into a position that you can pull cleanly, to score slightly above your average score. In doing this you avoid wild shots, and many times you get off practically on center.

A good score is not made by a large number of perfect shots, but by the absence of poor ones. It does not pay to try to pull centers, unless nothing else will do in a tight place; then be careful. If the sights will not settle before you begin to feel short of breath, put the rifle down and breathe very slowly and deeply 2 or 3 times; swallow and try again. Be sure you pull on a slow swing and with a perfectly clean pull.

The trigger should not be extremely light, but should be perfectly clean and without kick to the finger when it lets go. The trigger guard or lever should bring the trigger finger into such a position that a long forward reach is not necessary. The thumb should be along the side of the stock - not over it; in fact, it should form a gauge to keep the trigger finger in such a position that it comes naturally onto the trigger. This position you must learn to shoot well; the finger cannot be away from the trigger when you want to fire, but in contact with it. The best way when aiming is to keep squeezing the trigger with the finger, then when the sight swings deep into the bull, a little harder touch lets it off. The object of doing that is to avoid sympathetic movements of the other fingers. It is very hard to make a quick movement of one finger without also moving the adjacent fingers more or less, which disturbs the aim.

In aiming the rifle (NRA standing position), the left arm should be along the side, the elbow resting on the hip bone if you are so built; if not, then along the side on the short ribs - not in front over the heart and stomach, which cramps the breathing and heart action. Regardless of position, NRA or Army, the right arm should have the elbow well up, not against the side; this pulls the chest open and gives the lungs more capacity; it also allows a straighter stock which shoots more uniformly than one with much drop.

BREATHING

It is extremely important that you pay careful attention to this. One should breathe slowly and deeply. Do not allow yourself to breathe fast, as that tends to make the pulse rapid, which in turn affects the aim. If one is shooting continuous scores with fixed ammunition, one is apt to get short of breath before the score is finished and the pulse goes up. This is because the blood is robbed of the necessary oxygen when holding the breath. We compensate for this by deep slow breathing, making the whole surface of the lungs work instead of the small portion in ordinary use. As I raise my rifle to aim, I lift it high and fill my lungs fully; as I begin to settle I breathe nearly empty, then as the aim begins to settle, breathe about half full and hold the breath until I fire; then at once begin breathing again deeply and slowly.

WEIGHT OF RIFLE

For the finest offhand shooting the rifle must be muzzle heavy. This is not, as most shooters suppose, wholly in the weight of the rifle, but is in the disposition of the weight. As much as possible should be in the barrel. Weight in the stock and buttplate is to be condemned. While it tends to balance the rifle when the same is carried free, its weight is entirely on the right shoulder in shooting and does not in any way change the weight supported on the left hand. In fact, the rifle at the shoulder is a second-class lever in which the power is the weight of the rifle concentrated at its center of gravity, which should be well beyond the left hand. The fulcrum is the shoulder, and the work is the weight held in the left hand. If the center of gravity is in front of the left hand, then the weight held in the left hand is greater than the rifle. If the center of gravity is behind the left hand, the weight will be less than that of the rifle.

It is necessary to hold a reasonable amount of weight on the left hand in order that the swing of the rifle may be slow and give one time to pull. If the weight resting on the left hand be the same, no matter what the actual weight of the rifle itself, the effort to move it will be the same. It is possible to build a rifle to weigh 12 or 20 lbs. and have it hold exactly the same. In other words, except to absorb recoil, the shooting weight of a rifle is not how heavy the rifle actually is but how that weight is distributed. Anyone can prove these facts for themselves, as I have done for many years to my customers, by simply holding the rifle by the buttplate so it will not overturn on a small platform scale, first weighing the rifle itself, then by supporting it at various places to see what the left hand actually holds, and not forgetting before you finish to tie a couple of pounds or so onto the buttplate in order to convince yourself that it has absolutely no effect on the weight held in the left hand, and therefore has no effect on the shooting balance of the rifle and no influence in slowing the movement of the muzzle in aiming.

STOCK

This should be as straight as possible to conform with comfort. The cheekpiece should be high enough so that when the eye is in line with the sights it presses firmly against the cheek, as this materially helps steady the rifle. The cheekpiece, if hollowed, should have no projection in front - but a straight run - for the rifle recoils an appreciable amount before the bullet leaves the muzzle, and any projection rolls the rifle as it drives back and disturbs the aim, and this drive-back and roll will vary with uneven holds; consequently, the bullet direction also varies and you get shots where you do not expect them. It is very important that the buttstock should be tight. A loose buttstock will scatter the shots badly.

TELESCOPE

This absolutely must be focused at the distance at which you intend to shoot. The eye lens should be focused first looking at a blank sheet of paper, or the clear sky, so the cross-hairs are dead black and distinct. This is never changed unless your eyesight changes. Focusing for distance is done with the object lens or intermediate lens only. Use plain paper or clear sky so there is no object seen to confuse you. It is probable that different people will require different eye adjustment as they would spectacles. Set the telescope, on or off the rifle, on something so it will point at the target and not move easily. Then look through it and move the eye around quickly in every direction as far as you can see clearly, and notice whether the cross-hairs appear to be stationary on the target; they should not appear to move at all. If they do, the telescope must be focused by loosening the front lens or the intermediate lens, moving it very slightly in or out until repeated trials show that the cross-hairs do not apear to move, then tighten it carefully and look again to be sure you did not move it in tightening. This is the only position that will give correct shooting. It also should be the position of clearest vision, but it matters really very little whether the vision is perfectly distinct or not, but the cross-hairs must be still.

In putting the glass onto the rifle, be sure that the tube is wiped clean where it bears on the sides and slightly greased. Be very sure that the mounts and blocks are absolutely clean where they come together and that they are carefully tightened; I use a dime for a screwdriver. This makes them sufficiently tight without strain.

Keep a careful record of the readings of your telescope on different ranges and on different guns; you will then have no trouble in shifting from one range or gun to another. Once in a while test your telescope and mounts to see that everything about it is secure. Place the gun on anything solid so you can see through the telescope which is supposed to be properly tightened on it, look through the telescope and at the same time tap on the tube with a pencil; you will see the cross-hairs jump at each tap, but they should come back each time to absolutely the same place. If they do not, something is loose, either with the mounts or inside the scope. This happens, and any decent shooting is then simply impossible, and a good gun and ammunition gets blamed instead of a faulty scope or mounts.

After each shot return your telescope to its proper position from which the recoil has jarred it. To do this never take hold of the rear end and pull it back, but place the left forefinger on the barrel ahead of the telescope and slide the finger gently to place. The telescope will then come back each time to its proper place.

THE PALM REST

The proper position is important. It should be neither too close to the receiver nor too far away. If too close, the left hand has to support too much weight; also movements of the holding arm move the muzzle too rapidly. In other words, the control is bad; also the excessive weight tires one sooner. It must not be forgotten that the weight the left hand is holding is generally considerably in excess of the rifle itself, due to the center of gravity of the rifle being outside of the support.

You may think a big fellow like you can hold as long as you like, but you can't do it. I am a little fellow, but I can shoot rings around most large shooters. It is not size and strength that count, but nerve and judgement. With these instructions and a lot of careful practice you can attain in a short time what it took me years to learn. Study these methods. Shoot all you can. Carefully note everything that you do, and you will find your work improving. Pay attention to details!

CHAPTER 13

REST SHOOTING*

by N. H. Roberts

There are two methods of ascertaining whether or not any rifle and cartridge gives good, fair, extra fine or poor accuracy at any range. The best, most scientific method of doing this is by testing the rifle in a "machine rest" such as is used in our arms and ammunition factories, in the Springfield Armory, Rock Island Arsenal, Frankfort Arsenal and other plants where arms and cartridges are manufactured for the government. The .30-06 Springfield rifles made at that armory and at Rock Island were tested in the most improved type of machine rest known as the "Woodworth cradle", designed by Mr. A. L. Woodworth, chief of the Experimental Division of Springfield Armory, which is a modification of the "Mann V-Rest" and the machine rest before used in the government armories. A machine rest of this type is far too expensive and requires a concrete base about 20 by 32 inches at the top, set five or six feet in the ground, on which the machine rest is mounted in order that it will be absolutely steady and without even the slightest movement or vibration.

Early in 1900, Mr. E. A. Leopold of Morristown, Pennsylvania, suggested to Dr. Franklin W. Mann that scientific experiments should be conducted to determine the behavior of bullets in flight at various ranges, which riflemen and our ordnance department really knew nothing about, except by

---

* Letter from N.H. Roberts, some of this material also apeared in May 1944, *Hunting and Fishing*.

theory only. Accordingly he and Dr. Mann commenced experimentation and study in rifle ballistics which were continued until Dr. Mann's death. These experiments accomplished remarkable results and developed methods which led to increased accuracy and velocity that had before been considered impossible. Mr. Leopold and Dr. Mann were many years in advance of their time in their knowledge of rifle ballistics and made discoveries in this line that science, the arms manufacturers and our ordnance department knew nothing about until they learned of the facts which these two expert rifle experimenters had discovered years before, through their intensive study and experiments, in intelligent, scientific machine rest shooting.

The riflemen of the world owe a debt of gratitude to Dr. Mann, Mr. Leopold, A. O. Niedner, and H. M. Pope for the experiments and discoveries in rifle ballistics which they made during the years mentioned. I have a record of the fact that in 1914, Dr. Mann obtained a velocity of practically 6,000 f.s. with a certain high power rifle and cartridge, as shown by the Mann chronograph, and Adolph O. Niedner was the only man who knew the caliber of the barrel and the type and weight of bullet used by Dr. Mann in obtaining this extreme velocity.

While the average rifleman cannot have a machine rest of the type before mentioned, he can have a Pope or Hubalek machine rest and mount this on a small concrete base set about three feet in the ground, extending about two feet above ground and having a top about 10 inches wide by 2 1/2 or 3 feet long to which a hardwood plank, 3 inches thick, the same size as the top of the concrete base, is securely bolted. Then the Pope machine rest is attached to this plank top, and with which careful riflemen can obtain practically as accurate results in testing rifles and ammunition as can be obtained with the "Woodworth cradle" machine rest. However, the cost of the Pope and Hubalek machine rest and the construction of a very solid concrete base on which to mount this, prevents its use by the great majority of riflemen.

The ordinary rifleman who has the use of a rifle range can construct a bench rest with which he can learn a great deal about the accuracy of a rifle, cartridges loaded with different kinds and charges of smokeless powder, different shapes and weights of bullets, as well as affording a very interesting and instructive sport. A good bench rest may be constructed from five spruce, or fir, posts about 42 inches long by 4 or 5 inches square. These posts are fastened together to make a rectangular, solid support of the top, by firmly nailing pieces 1 1/2 inches thick by 4 inches wide, even with the top of the posts and the fifth leg supporting the arm rest. A top is then made of two pieces of spruce, or fir, plank 2 inches thick by 10 inches wide and 32 inches long and one piece of the same thickness and width but 48 or 52 inches long, which are firmly attached, by wire spikes, to the legs and arm rest. Of course, the top of the rest should be made of dressed planks, planed smooth on both sides and the edges of the planks fitted closely together so as to form a nice smooth top. The 48 or 52 inch plank of the top is nailed firmly in place on the right hand side of the rest and projects 16 or 18 inches back of the other two pieces, to form a rest for the right arm when shooting. The other two planks are spiked in place on top of the four legs to make the rest of the top and to provide space for setting up the spotting scope and places for boxes of cartridges, notebook, etc.

The five legs should be firmly set about 12 inches in the ground, after the top has been nailed in place, and the legs further braced and strengthened by nailing pieces 1 1/2 inches thick by 4 inches wide firmly to all five legs about four inches above the ground. A stool, or bench, about 18 inches is then made for the shooter to sit on when shooting. Then a rectangular box, without ends, is made of 1 inch lumber to form a rest 10 inches long, 7 or 8 inches wide and 8 or 9 inches high, on which the aluminum muzzle clamp rests and slides with the recoil when shooting. The top of this box should be planed perfectly smooth and kept so in order that the muzzle clamp will slide freely on it when shooting. This arrangement provides a solid bench rest 30 inches high at which the rifleman sits with his right side against the left edge of the arm rest plank, his body leaning against the rear edge of the table, while the muzzle of the rifle, with the muzzle clamp attached, rests on the box-like support and keeps the rifle from canting. The shooter places his left hand under the butt of the rifle, with the back of his hand down, on the arm rest and adjusts the rifle for elevation and aligning the sights on the bull's-eye; then he carefully squeezes the trigger without moving the rifle and thus learns whether or not his bullet struck the point aimed at. If the bullet did not hit the point of aim, he corrects the elevation or windage before firing the next shot, and by looking through the spotting scope after each shot, the rifleman can see just where each bullet hit the target when shooting at 100 or 200 yards, without having a man at the target to mark the shots. Instead of placing the left hand, back down, under the stock to get the elevation and steady the rifle, a wedge-shaped block of wood may be placed under the stock to give the right adjustment of the sights, or scope, on the target. This wedge-block should be about 10 inches long, 3 inches wide, 1/2 inch thick at one end and 1 3/4 inches thick at the other; in use it is placed with the thick end towards the trigger guard; thus supporting the rifle solidly and uniformly. When the wedge-block is used in this way in rest shooting, it is called "double rest shooting" since the rifle is supported, or rested, in two places - near the muzzle by the muzzle clamp and the stock resting on the wedge-block under it.

No living man can hold a rifle steady enough, even when shooting in the prone position, to be absolutely sure that he did not move the rifle, slightly at least, when the shot was fired; but when shooting from a bench rest and using the muzzle and arm rest described, a careful man can soon learn to shoot practically as accurately in this way as with a machine rest. Shooting from a bench rest is the most comfortable position, as well as the steadiest, in which a rifle may be shot and by this method the rifleman can ascertain just which kind and charge of powder and which type and weight of bullets really give the best accuracy in his individual rifle. He can also, after having some experience in bench rest shooting, determine for himself whether any certain caliber of rifle and cartridge give the better average accuracy at 100, 200 or 300 yards than some other rifle. Very often a rifleman who uses only factory loaded cartridges in his rifle, desires to find out whether Western, Winchester, Remington or Peters cartridges, all loaded with the same weight and kind of bullets, give the best accuracy in his rifle, and this may be determined accurately by firing five shots of each kind of cartridges from the bench rest at 100 or 200 yards, or more; then measuring each group. Having made this test himself, with his own rifle, he knows just which make of cartridges actually are the most accurate in his rifle instead of believing what some other shooter tells him about this matter.

In testing a hunting rifle from bench rest, take a cloth bag, about the size of a 25 pound sugar bag, fill it with fine, dry sand free from small stones, tie the neck tightly to keep the sand in, and place this sand bag on the bench rest. Then rest the fore-arm of the rifle, about two inches from the end, on the sand bag, place the left hand under the butt of the rifle, or grasp the fore-arm with the left hand and rest it on the sand bag; then fire the rifle while being careful not to move it as the trigger is squeezed. Five shots carefully fired in this way will show the average accuracy of that rifle and enable the shooter to correctly adjust the sights for the desired range. A rifle fired in this way from sand bag rest will give the same point of impact of the bullets on the target as when shot off-hand, or in the sitting or prone positions.

The man especially who hand loads his cartridges needs some kind of a bench rest from where he can test cartridges having various kinds and charges of powder and different weights, shapes and kinds of bullets, in order that he may really determine just which powder and charge and type and weight of these bullets really give the best accuracy - make the smallest groups - at 100 or 200 yards. Then, having determined this matter, he can adopt a "standard load and bullet" for his individual rifle with the assurance that the cartridges thus loaded give the very best accuracy obtainable with his rifle.

The use of a good bench rest will save many times its costs in determining the most accurate charge and kind of smokeless powder to use with any bullet in any caliber of rifle, in correctly adjusting the sights of a rifle with any cartridge, teach the rifleman the importance of seeing the sights and target exactly alike each and every time he shoots, and thus increase his skill in off-hand shooting, not decrease his skill as some shooters think.

Bronze cast re-de capper for bench use. Maker unknown.

Powder measures left to right: (1) Schoyen single cavity measure, reconstructed by John Jamieson from original parts. (2) Schoyen-Peterson glass powder holders duplex measure, measured a priming charge and a main load, sliding bar principal. (3) A. O. Bremer, San Francisco, California duplex powder measure. (4) D. W. King, Jr., Denver, Colorado, the finest made of the duplex powder measures.

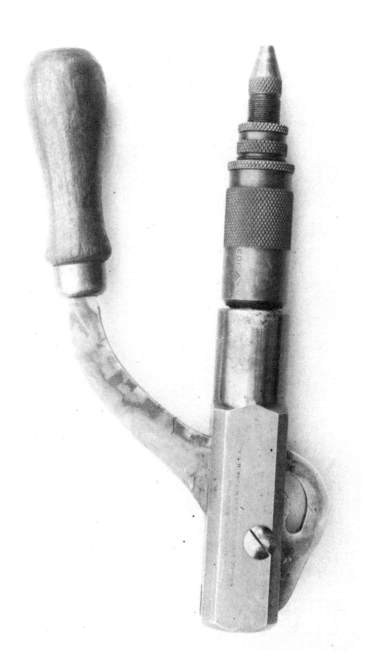

.303 Savage reloading tool showing very high grade of workmanship.

Black jappaned tin, hand soldered powder can containing one pound of black powder. This bears the Sharps Rifle Co. label and was sold by the company. The powder was packaged but not made by Sharps. *This photo also appears on the front cover.*

Schuetzen and #1 powder cans formerly owned and used by Charles C. Rowland of Boulder, Colo. now in possession of G. O. Kelver.

Schuetzen duplex powder measure made by the Milwaukee Brass Works of Milwaukee, Wisconsin. Coll. John Dutcher, Colo.

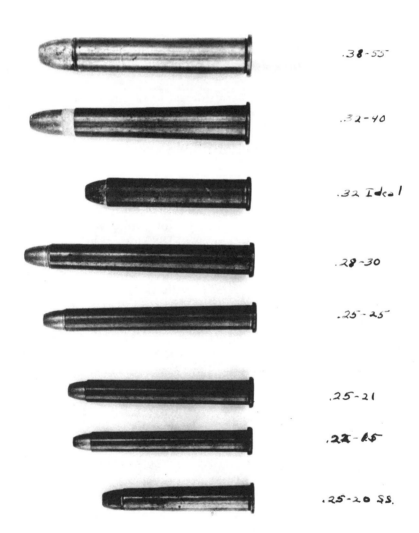

.38-55

.32-40

.32 Ideal

.28-30

.25-25

.25-21

.25-15

.25-20 SS.

Schuetzen Rifle Cartridges.

ADDENDA

Rifle telescopes were not mass-produced until around the turn of the century. Even the best of the early makers produced only ten or twelve telescopes a year.

William Malcom was considered to be the most knowledge-able of the early telescope makers. He, along with L. M. Mogg of Marcellus, New York, J. W. Sidle, and Milton P. Pierce of Philadel-phia, Pennsylvania, produced rifle telescopes for use by the Union forces during the Civil War, 1861-65.

Later, Malcom along with J. R. Chapman, a civil engineer, Morgan James, rifleman and gunmaker; and Charles A. Spencer an optician, began experimenting to improve the rifle telescope.

Their findings indicated that a long tube telescope had less errors than shorter tubes. The 1870-1880 long tube telescope was based on their findings.

Hunting telescopes did not become practical until William Malcolm discovered the use of the intermediate lens in the early 1870's. The discovery permitted the concentration of light within the lens system.

The first short tube rifle telescope was produced by William Malcolm for a Dr. Perry of New York, in 1884. The tube was 12 inches long and the resolution was a marvel of the optical world.

The development of the contained eye piece by Fred L. Smith for the Stevens Arms Company in the early 1900's permitted further development and shortened tube lengths.

The Civil War telescopes all had similar primitive telescope mountings and adjustments.

The Malcolm and the Mogg telescopes looked very similar, these telescopes had the windgauge adjustment in the front mount and the elevation in the rear mount.

Gerald O. Kelver

RELOADING TOOLS, SIGHTS, AND TELESCOPES
for Single Shot Rifles

SECOND PRINTING 1990

Because of the continued demand and interest in this book, it has been decided to make a second printing with added material relevant to both collecting and using the instruments related to the shooting of single shot rifles.

————————

CONTENTS 1990 SECOND PRINTING .... PAGE

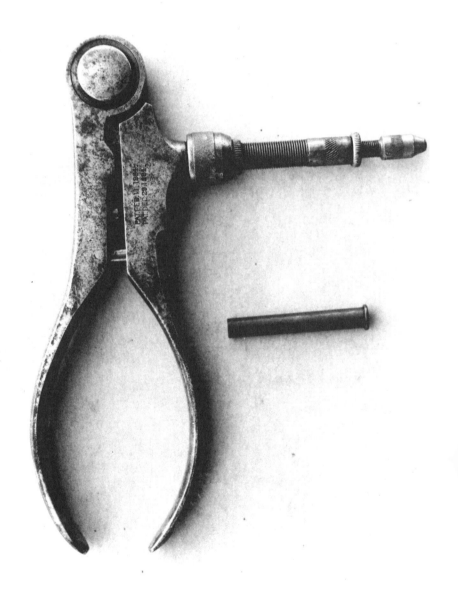

IDEAL 1884 TONG TOOL

Pictured is a standard Ideal tong tool for the .25-21 Stevens and adjustable to take the .25-25 Stevens cartridges.

There appears to be nothing unusual about this tool and it is the standard factory production item; however, if you examine the method of attaching and adjusting the double adjustable chamber, you will note a very unusual knurled nut which is threaded to the tool. The tool has a male thread and the nut threads on to this and the double adjustable chamber threads into the nut.

This is a factory product, but I have only seen this method of fastening the double adjustable chamber to the tong tool on this one.

There are variations even among the common tools.

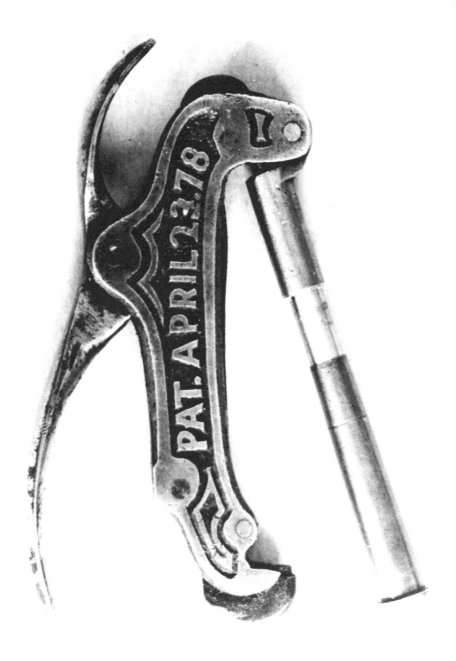

Hugh A. Kingsland of Newark, New Jersey patent of April 23, 1878 hand held de- and re-capping tool.

HUGH A. KINGSLAND
RE & DE CAPPER 1878

One of the many hand held implements for capping and de-capping the cartridge case was one developed by Hugh A. Kingsland of Newark, New Jersey who patented his device on April 23, 1878. His patent papers were originally filed March 1, 1878. Patent paper number is 202831.

The finding of any hand held capping-de-capping tools is strictly one of chance, for the tools were discarded by persons not knowing what they were and caring less.

In almost every case of finding these tools I have found them in what could be called the "junk boxes" at the gun shows because I knew what I was looking at, although sometimes the tool might be a puzzle because of missing parts. The comments apply to all the re-de-cappers, not just this tool.

The body of the tool is of cast bronze as is the cartridge case holding rod. The handles and the rocking recapper are of iron.

Pressure by the palm of the hand on the short handle cases the re-capper rod to withdraw from the case anchor and the pin inside the cartridge holding rod is activated and the primer is expelled. Pressure on the longer handle causes the recapper to seat the primer.

This particular tool has a case rod marked "40", but the rod has been lathe turned at a later date to handle the .32-40 case. The .40 caliber rifles were the most popular when the tool was originally developed. The tool will handle a .40-70 case.

The tool was originally painted green and sides polished to show the brass. On one side is the patent date April 23, 78 and on the other is a full length rifle in raised brass.

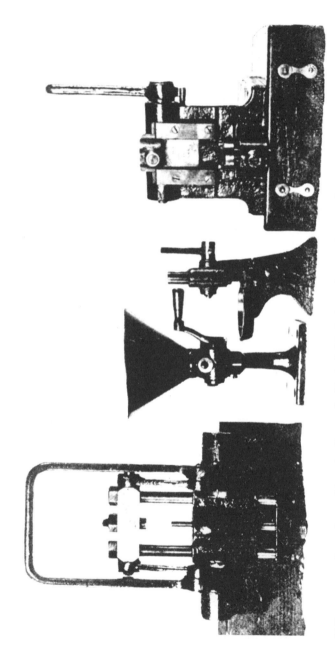

Full government barracks cartridge reloading outfit. To the left is the levered case resizer, powder measure, re-capper, and bullet seater with the box for the accessories.

U. S. MILITARY
RELOADING TOOLS

One type of reloading tools which are not usually discussed are the U.S. Government reloading tools. These tools have not been available since the early 1920's when many sets were sold to the National Rifle Association members through the Director of Civilian Marksmanship for $36.13 plus the shipping charges.

The reloading sets which were sold at that time were marked Frankford Arsenal 1907 and were for the .30-40 Krag and the .30-1906 cartridges. Previous sets had been available to the armed services in .45-70 Government. The tools were bench type tools with heavy cast frames that could be screwed or bolted to a bench.

There was no powder scale, no bullet mold, nor bullet sizer-lubricator.

The finish on the tools was of high quality and more like the fine workmanship and finish on an old fashioned Winchester than the usual reloading tool finish of the commercial production.

The set was made up of the following items:
- 1 - recapper and accessories in a wood cabinet
- 1 - set of dies, gauges, wrenches, and small parts in a wood cabinet
- 1 - resizing press
- 1 - bullet seating press
- 1 - recapping press
- 1 - de-capping hand held tool
- 1 - powder measure

The two case resizing dies were for the .30-40 and .30'06 cases as were the cartridge length dies and diameter gauges.

There was a brass die cleaning rod, two double end hair bristle cleaning brushes, a round flat oil can, two small rod punches, two seven inch screwdrivers and one nine inch monkey wrench.

The powder measure worked similarly to an Ideal #5 measure. The adjustment, however, was decidedly different, for in the powder cavity was a nut which had to be screwed one way or the other to get the adjustment needed to the powder charge. This adjustment was made by inserting the special little wrench up through the discharge drop tube and making the adjustment to the powder charge adjusting nut.

The measure threw 59 grains of DuPont #20 powder as a maximum charge and 23 grains of #20 as a minimum charge. The charge cylinder was easily removed for it slid out to one side like the Ideal measure. The powder hopper on the measure was made of heavy tin and shaped like a funnel.

The case resizing press operated well, but a longer handle would give more leverage. This press was years ahead of its time and only comparatively recently has anything of its equal appeared as a commercial press. The case sizing dies were in two parts, and by reversing the correct position of the neck die and machining a slight bevel so the case would start true, a better fitting neck sizing operation could be accomplished.

The hand held decapping tool is handy and fast operating once the operator gets the hang of it.

The recapping tool is speedy and reliable; it is about six inches high and operates like a miniature arbor press.

The bullet seater operates smoothly although from its appearance it looks like a lot of tool. The seater does not support the case in a die while seating the bullet, which is unfortunate.

The U.S. Government reloading tools are of primary interest to collectors of U.S. military items; however, as tools used in the reloading of cartridges their existence should not be ignored.

1903 - TOOL FOR DE-CAPPING AND RE-CAPPING CARTRIDGE SHELLS

When I originally wrote the material for *Reloading Tools, Sights, and Telescopes for Single Shot Rifles,* I attributed a lever action type .45-70 re and de-capper to the Denver A. W. Peterson shop. Similarly made parts to the tool were in the old Peterson shop when it was disbanded. A distinctive tool had also been made by Peterson and later by John Jamieson of Denver that had a scissor type movement to actuate the tool.

One of the Steven-Pope re and de-cappers in the Tom Dunn, Casper, Wyoming collection also intrigued me for it had a patent date on one of the handles of September 15, 1903.

I attempted to get information regarding this patent, but if you have had any experience with the U.S. Patent Office you know what a frustrating experience that can be and with no results.

Later I read that Robert Sears of the National Rifle Association staff had also been investigating the same patent but with more success: Mr. Sears found that the Stevens-Pope patent date referred to Patent #739,151 dated September 15, 1903 and issued to a Martines Chick of San Diego, California with an assignor of one-half to Harvey McMurchy of Fulton, New York. The patent papers note that no model was with the patent request.

The tool which I own and which was pictured as a Peterson tool, when laid beside the patent papers is obviously a drawing of the tool itself.

Here we have a puzzle of a patentee in California, a gunsmith in Denver, Colorado who either made a similar, or copied, the original tool, and a manufacturer in Chicopee Falls, Massachusetts acknowledging the existence of the patent on a manufactured product.

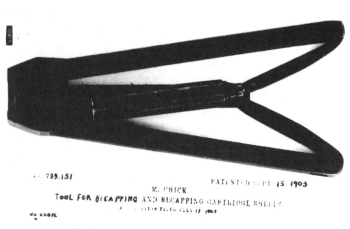

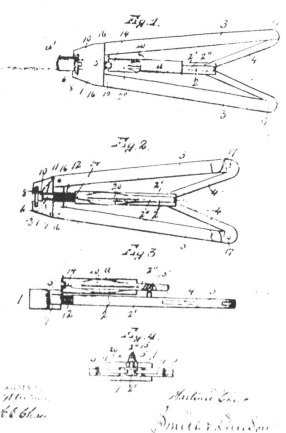

M. Chick .45-70 reloading tool patented Sept. 15, 1903 with the patent paper drawings.

The survival rate of the small hand held re-de-cappers and loading tools has been very small, and this particular tool, along with many others will furnish material for discussion and further research for a long time to come.

Both Stevens Arms Co. and Schoyen-Peterson shop made payments to the patentees for the use of the patent. Oddly the payments for the use of the patent ceased after a few years. I can find no court jurisdiction in regard to the patent, but perhaps more clarification will be revealed at some future date.

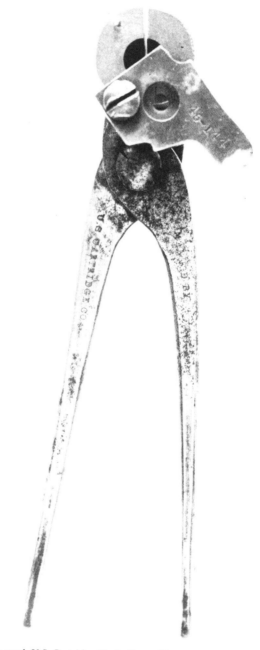

.40 caliber paper patch U.S. Cartridge Co. bullet mold.

U. S. CARTRIDGE CO., LOWELL, MASS., RELOADING TOOLS

In the March 10, 1881 issue of *Forest and Stream* is a report of a reloading accident using U.S. Cartridge Company tools. The injured person was reloading cartridges for a Springfield musket, caliber .45. The details leading up to the explosion were given and the question was raised as to why the explosion occurred.

The *Forest and Stream* editor's comments followed and he suggested several possibilities for the cause of the accident, then he made the statement, "Certain it is that the arrangements have been used thousands of times at all posts of the U.S. Army and a similar accident has not come to our ears."

I had not been aware that the U.S. Cartridge Company reloading tools were used as extensively by the U.S. Army as this article would seem to indicate. Further research regarding these tools might prove enlightening.

For myself, I have a well-made iron mold casting a paper patch bullet which is marked on one handle "Made By" and on the other "U.S. Cartridge Co."

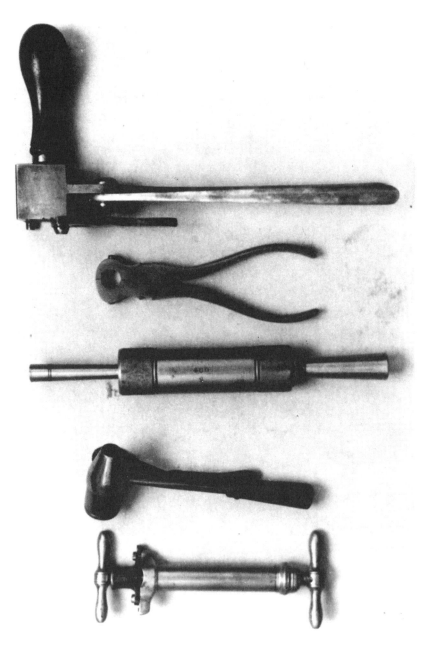

Rifle tools included in an English single shot rifle case of the 1870-1900's. From left to right: Reprimer and

ENGLISH RIFLE TOOLS

Many fine English single shot rifles were used in the United States during the 1870-1900 period. Today it is very rare to find one of these cased rifles with all the tools.

English rifle tools were not made by the one who assembled the rifle, but were made to specifications by various makers and then included in the casing as part of the rifle.

This particular rifle is one made by Alexander Henry of Edinburg, Scotland. The tools consist of a gold plated cartridge crimping tool to provide a base in the case for the bullet to seat upon, and a gold plated screw type recapper and bullet seater chamber.

The spring lever powder measure is for a full charge of black powder. There is a well made hand cartridge resizing die and a hollow point bullet mold for casting the bullets.

The set also contains a steel arch punch for cutting the felt, cardboard, or cork wads which were placed over the powder prior to seating the paper patched bullet in the cartridge case.

There is also a cleaning rod and cleaning devices included in the case. When one traveled the case always was used to house the gun and everything was included in the case to make the rifle shoot and for its maintenance.

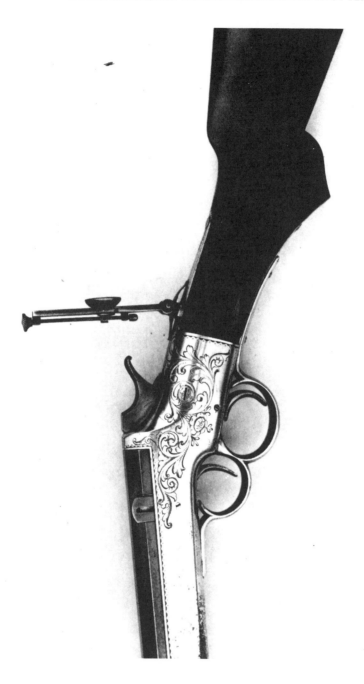

Frank Wesson engraved rifle with fine Wesson vernier tang sight. Collection of John Maddux, Colorado.

F. WESSON
TARGET RIFLE SIGHT

On page 107 of this book information is recorded concerning the American maker of distinctive firearms.

This picture will show the fine workmanship and detail of one of his better quality arms.

Note the well made tang sight which has the bowed staff spring between the staff and base. This method of keeping the staff in position was also used in the J. M. Marlin Ballard sight.

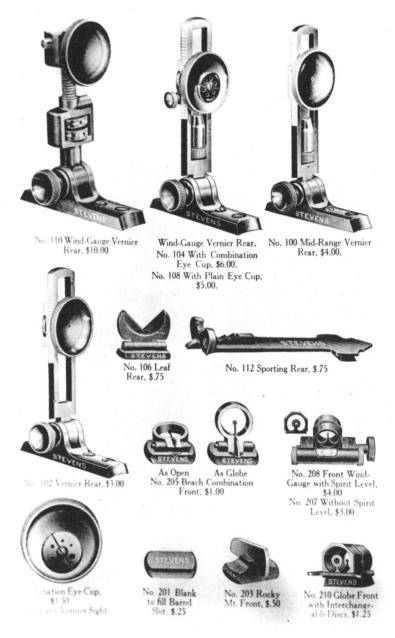

No. 110 Wind-Gauge Vernier Rear, $10.00

Wind-Gauge Vernier Rear. No. 104 With Combination Eye Cup, $6.00. No. 108 With Plain Eye Cup, $5.00.

No. 100 Mid-Range Vernier Rear, $4.00.

No. 106 Leaf Rear, $.75

No. 112 Sporting Rear, $.75

No. 102 Vernier Rear, $3.00

As Open   As Globe No. 205 Beach Combination Front, $1.00

No. 208 Front Wind-Gauge with Spirit Level, $4.00 No. 207 Without Spirit Level, $3.00

Combination Eye-Cup, $1.50 Rotary Vernier Sight

No. 201 Blank to fill Barrel Slot, $.25

No. 203 Rocky Mt. Front, $.50

No. 210 Globe Front with Interchangeable Discs, $1.25

J. Stevens Arms & Tool Co., Chicopee Falls, Mass. Catalog #53, 1911; illustrating sights and combination sighting discs.

COMBINATION
SIGHT DISC OR EYE CUP

The combination eye cup is a standard sighting disc which has been fitted with an inner device which permits the rapid selection of the proper peep by the shooter. The original sight disc for many years carried a screw held disc with the choice of six peep holes. Later discs carried an arm arrangement which permitted the choice of three different sight peeps.

The idea was to provide for the different conditions of light in one sight disc obviating the necessity of carrying a selection of different size discs.

The J. Stevens Arms Co. of Chicopee Falls, Massachusetts was the first company to offer this combination sighting disc as a standard option to the sights furnished for their target firearms.

This Combination Eye Cup was offered in the 1898 J. Stevens Arms and Tool Co. catalog and continued to be offered through the 1939 catalog.

This combination sight disc or eye cup was preferred by target shooters whenever iron sights were required. The disc was also offered as an accessory item by other sight makers and was used by many small bore shooters after 1940. It is today one of the preferred sighting aids for iron sights.

BREATHING TUBES
FOR POWDER FOULING

A "Dolan" breathing tube was a light full barrel length tube with a small funnel on one end which could be used as a mouthpiece, usually nickle plated, and made to fit the particular bore of the rifle.

The shooter used this tube to blow moist breath into the tube and the bore of the rifle to soften the black powder fouling. Supposedly this moistened the fouling enough to permit the bullet to clear out the fouling on its passage down the barrel. This procedure was recommended if cleaning between shots was not possible.

The Sharps Rifle Company included these special tubes with their loading tools for the years of 1878-'79 and '80 for use in their long range rifles.

These tubes could also be inserted into the barrel after the empty reprimed cartridge case was inserted in the breech and the breech closed. The measured black powder charge was then poured down the tube giving a more compact and uniform loading due to the long tube drop.

These tubes are now rarely found for the tubes enjoyed a very short period of popularity. Very rarely these tubes could be found with black powder schuetzen rifles in .32-40 and .38-55, although I have not seen one for many years.

BIBLIOGRAPHY

Amber, John, *Gun Digest Treasury*, Gun Digest Co., Chicago, Ill. 1956

American Field, Chicago, Ill. 3-8-1884 issue.

American Rifleman, 1600 Rhode Island Ave. N.W., Washington, D.C. Dec. 1941, July 1961, March 1964, December 1967.

Bullard Arms Co., Springfield, Mass. Catalog, 1887-88.

Curry, N. & Bro., 113 Sansome St., San Francisco, Calif. Catalog, 1884.

Donaldson, H.A. Letters 1935-37. Files of Tom Axtell, Oakville, Washington.

Frasca, Albert J., and Hill, Robert H., *45-70 Springfield*, Springfield Pub. Co., Northridge, Calif. 1980.

Gould, A.C. *Modern American Rifles*, Bradee Whidden Co. Boston, Mass. 1892.

Government Printing Office, *Publication No. 1990, Description of De-Capping and Cleaning Tools for Samll Arms Cartridges*. Washington, D.C. 1917.

Handbooks, Ideal, Ideal mfg. Co., New Haven, Conn. Ideal Handbooks #7 to #34.

Kelver, Gerald O., *Schuetzen Rifles History and Loadings*, Published by G.O. Kelver, Brighton, Colo. 1972.

Kelver, Gerald O., *Respectfully Yours, H.M. Pope*, published by G.O. Kelver, Brighton, Colo. 1976.

Lyman Gunsight Co. Middlefield, Conn. Catalogs and handbooks.

Lyman Centennial Jouranl 1878-1978, Lyman Publications, Middlefield, CT. 1978.

Mann, Franklin W., *The Bullet's Flight*, Standard Printing and Publishing Co., Huntington W. Va. 1908.

Marlin Firearms Co., New Haven, Conn. Catalog, 1888.

Mass. Arms co., Chicopee Falls, Mass. Catalog, 1880.

Redfield, Watt & Turner, Robert. Unpublished manuscript. *A History of the Redfield Family in Oregon and of John H. Redfield, Founder of the Redfield Gun Sight Co.* 1965

Remington U.M.C. Arms Co., Ilion, N.Y. Catalogs 1877-1882.

Stevens, J. Arms and Tool Co., Chicopee Falls, Mass. Catalogs 1884-1913.

Turner, Robert. "John H. Redfield He Hit His Mark". *Shooting Times*. Peoria Journal Star, Inc. News Plaza, Peoria, Ill. 61601. October, 1965.

Whitney Arms Co., New Haven, Conn. Catalog, 1878.

Winchester Repeating Arms Co., New Haven, Conn. Catalogs 1891-1914.